Posters from the Collection of The Museum of Modern Art
Selected and edited by Mildred Constantine
Text by Alan M. Fern

The Museum of Modern Art, New York
Distributed by New York Graphic Society Ltd., Greenwich, Connecticut

Published with the assistance of CBS Foundation, Inc.
Copyright © 1968, The Museum of Modern Art
11 West 53 Street, New York, New York 10019
Library of Congress Catalogue Card Number 68–54920
Designed by Massimo Vignelli, Pieter van Delft/Unimark International
Type set by Graphic Arts Typographers, Inc.
Printed in the U.S.A. by Davis-Delaney-Arrow, Inc.
Bound by Sendor Bindery, Inc.
Jacket printed by MacNaughton Lithograph Company Inc.

In *Ulysses* the free-lance advertising salesman, Leopold Bloom, wanders the city in search of "some one sole unique advertisement to cause passers to stop in wonder, a poster novelty, with all extraneous accretions excluded, reduced to its simplest and most efficient terms not exceeding the span of casual vision and congruous with the velocity of modern life." Here is a cogent and perhaps ironic definition of the poster, embodying the criteria by which the form is usually assessed. But what raises the poster above such short-lived impact, what raises its finest examples to the level of art, is the magic of its elements intentionally simplified, summing up the aesthetic aspirations of the times, and even leading to new kinds of visual experience. It is the development of the poster as an art form over the past century that is described and illustrated in this book, with outstanding examples ranging from the powerful lithographs of Chéret, Bonnard, and Lautrec to the "psychedelic" brilliance and technical ingenuity of today's experimenters.

As Alan Fern suggests, the history of the traditional poster – a two-dimensional design combining word and image on a printed sheet – may be coming to an end. Paradoxically this change is taking place at the same time as, and partly as a result of, an upsurge of popular interest, a poster boom embracing the artists who design them and the new audience that collects them. There are still posters produced in the shadow of the earlier tradition, but one departure has been the appearance of posters as "cult objects," with no purpose or cause beyond themselves; they have meaning without message, like the *nouvelle vague* cinema without a plot. The popularity of posters attests, in fact, to a greater involvement between the artists and their public than ever before. While the poster of the past was made almost entirely for public display and was preserved only by a few collectors, today the environment surrounding the young has given the poster a new audience and new places to be shown – in their own rooms, in campus halls, in casual art galleries and stores. The poster has recently become a public art, printed in thousands rather than hundreds, and sold at prices ranging from less than a dollar to several hundred dollars. The current interest in posters, moreover, is not limited to present production, but has also aroused among collectors and institutions fresh interest and enthusiasm in the art form as it developed in the past.

In the nineteenth century, industrial and social revolution gave printed matter a new meaning; advertising changed its function from information to persuasion. This function still applies in the present when products, ideas, or even political candidates are to be "sold," but in recent years the very proliferation of printed images has made them less effective, together with the increasing impact of the moving forms, biting into the eye, of films, and the immediacy of television. Partly as a result of this, partly as an aspect of the general ferment in contemporary art, there is a restless, exciting exploration of form and process occupying artists on virtually every continent. Sometimes these works are designed by individuals, sometimes by group manufacture. Wrestling with new techniques, many of these artists use the same elements of expression interchangeably in posters, prints, paintings – even sculpture and design objects. Printing is not merely a means for duplicating the artist's design; the artist has entered the shop, and the printing process itself has become one of his tools. These artists do not render history the homage of rejection; they freely use the styles of the past and adapt them to their own vocabularies. Another aspect of this spirit of involvement and change is the increasing willingness of artists to undertake posters of social commitment – a commitment surpassing that even of the thirties. Some of their works command attention by their aesthetic merit; many, admittedly, are less valuable as works of art than as inflammatory social documents, however avidly they are collected.

Over the past hundred years the vision and achievement of artists have been a source and catalyst for much of our everyday environment. Today, however, there is evidence of a reversal of the usual filtered-down process of form and style from the fine to the popular arts. In particular, the vocabulary, style, and force of the poster – a popular art if ever there was one – influence the other arts of our time.

This book, as well as the exhibition of the same name shown at The Museum of Modern Art early in 1968, is based on the Museum's own graphic design collection, which had its genesis with that of the Museum itself in 1929. It has been administered by the Department of Architecture and Design since the 1930's, first under Philip Johnson and then Arthur Drexler. The encouragement and support of Alfred H. Barr, Jr., Monroe Wheeler, and the late René d'Harnoncourt were also vital to its growth. The collection now consists of more than 2,000 posters and related works, selected primarily for their aesthetic quality, but also including work of mainly historical or social significance.

The Museum has shown more than 35 exhibitions of posters and other forms of graphic design, and has sponsored several competitions in an effort to encourage designers, civic institutions, printers, and the public to raise graphic design standards in this country. With the establishment of the Philip Goodwin Gallery of Architecture and Design in 1964, it became possible to keep at least a small part of the collection on permanent view. The remainder is now accessible for study in the Museum's recently established Lillie P. Bliss International Study Center. Anticipated expansion of the Museum's galleries will allow the continuous exhibition of a substantial part of the collection.

Many artists, collectors, galleries, and museums have given works to the collection. An exchange program with the Library of Congress, the Victoria and Albert Museum, the Stedelijk Museum in Amsterdam, the Musée des Arts Décoratifs in Paris, and the Glasgow Institute of Fine Arts, has also brought many major works into the collection. Finally, particular thanks should go to certain individuals who have made significant contributions of works and who have established purchase funds: Mr. and Mrs. Alfred H. Barr, Jr., Mr. and Mrs. Armand P. Bartos, the late Holger Cahill, the late Ludwig Charell, Mr. and Mrs. Arthur A. Cohen, the late Bernard Davis, the late Harold Davis, Mr. and Mrs. Leo Farland, the late A. Conger Goodyear, Joseph H. Heil, Mr. and Mrs. H. Lawrence Herring, Phyllis B. Lambert, Jay Leyda, Gertrud A. Mellon, the late Peter Muller-Munk, Lillian Nassau, Don Page, Mrs. Stanley Resor, the late Abby Aldrich Rockefeller, John D. Rockefeller 3rd, Nelson A. Rockefeller, G. E. Kidder Smith, Sydney S. Spivack, Paul Standard, and Benjamin Weiss.

M.C.

Over the years the Museum has issued several small publications on posters, usually in connection with exhibitions. *Word and Image* was the first comprehensive exhibition of the graphic design collection, and this book is the Museum's first comprehensive publication devoted to the subject. A great many people contributed to its preparation, giving generously of their time and ideas. Special thanks are due to John Garrigan of the Department of Architecture and Design; to Edgar Breitenbach and Elena Gonzalez of Prints and Photographs Division of the Library of Congress; to Wolf von Eckhardt, James Truitt, and Wanda Corn; to Bernard Karpel and the staff of the Museum Library; to Gray Williams, Françoise Boas, and Christie Kaiser of the Publications Department; and to the book's designers Massimo Vignelli and Pieter van Delft.

M.C. and A.F.

Contents

In the latter half of the nineteenth century two ancient forms of communication –
writing and pictures – joined recent developments in the technology of printing to
create the printed pictorial poster. At first this was a frivolous invention,
dedicated primarily to advertising the glories of Parisian cafés and entertainers;
but very quickly the poster became so potent a force in the formation and
transmission of artistic style that it transcended its original purpose and began to
affect all the visual arts.

This book is a brief history of the modern poster (and its close typographical
relatives) as an art form. The history of advertising is fascinating, but since it
contains many chapters of negligible aesthetic interest, it is not my subject.

I have limited my investigations to those designers who have approached the poster
as a means of expression as well as communication, and have explored graphic
design and typography as serious creative media.

One of the major accomplishments of these graphic artists has been the
confirmation of the aesthetic significance of typographical forms: that is, the
realization that letters can be formal design elements as well as basic symbols of
communication. The presence of typographic motifs in the paintings and
collages of Picasso, Braque, and Schwitters are early testimony to the power of
this idea: today the use of a Campbell's soup label, a Brillo box, or a stenciled
message carries the same recognition into art of a different sort. The
cross-fertilization of the arts traditionally considered "pure" with the design of
posters and graphic ephemera must command most of our attention in the
account that follows, for it is this that justifies our treating the subject with all the
solemnity and care usually reserved for painting and sculpture.

There are several characteristics of our own day that invite comparison with the
1890's, which for all practical purposes is the beginning of this history. Through
posters many important painters of the nineties became involved with the
graphic arts, while at the same time retaining their free style of working. Others
came to the poster from typography or the decorative arts. Thus two basic
approaches – that of the *artist* and that of the *designer* – were established. They
have existed, side by side, ever since. Even more important, the posters of the
nineties were crucial in bringing avant-garde painting into contact with the
decorative arts, resulting in the combustible style of Art Nouveau. Graphic design
has served a similar catalytic function since, and does so today.

Poster collecting in the 1890's reached the proportions of a mania; today, there
are countless collectors of posters, and shops that cater to their desires. The
printing of extra copies of posters intended for specific advertising campaigns
was common then, and is common now; it is not unusual for a poster to be
designed for sale – and not advertise a thing. Chéret did this 70 years ago;
designers are doing it today.

In the nineties the technology of lithographic printing had been brought to a high state of refinement, and the introduction of power-driven presses, mechanical typesetting devices, and efficient techniques of photoengraving were exerting a revolutionary impact on printing. Today, photo-typesetting, highly sophisticated offset lithography, silk screen, and other color printing developments of great flexibility are again causing a technological revolution. Such considerations as these may suggest why, although printing had been around for hundreds of years, graphic design was a child of the late nineteenth century. Coupled to technological advance was a great increase in leisure and wealth that fostered the development of the industries of entertainment and advertising – both essential to the poster artist and graphic designer. Moreover, the discovery that advertising techniques could also be propaganda techniques called the poster artist into the service of war and revolution – two facts of life in every decade of our century so far.

Today, we are in a period of new exploration of the potentialities of the graphic arts, and perhaps the work of our time will seem to critics of the future as radical and seminal as that of the 1890's does to us today. We take for granted that graphic design in general and the poster in particular will be used to arrest the eye, to inform in a direct manner, and to convey a clear sense of meaning or emotion. Let us begin by turning back to a time when these premises were not so generally conceded, and when the graphic arts were still stepchildren of commercial printing.

"I am bent on doing all I can with a first attempt at what I consider might develop into a most important branch of art," wrote the British artist Fred Walker around 1871.[1] Walker was at work on his first and only poster design (page 13), advertising Wilkie Collins' novel *The Woman in White.* His statement was more prophetic than his poster, as it turned out, but his design is characteristic of the best that the public could expect to find on the streets in the 1860's and 1870's. Essentially it consists of an illustration accompanied by lettering. His bold drawing, reproduced in black and white, is closely related to the later work of the pre-Raphaelites, but bears little relationship to the text.

If this was the high art of the poster, other designs – related in conception – were even less well conceived. Elaborately humorous drawings, complicated and cluttered typography announced a profusion of soaps, publications, and patent medicines in Great Britain, the United States, and France. In France the exceptions to this rule were perhaps of a higher level – one thinks of the Manet cats and Tony Johannot's *Don Quichotte* (page 13) — but even these works were scarcely able to point out a new direction in graphic design through the morass of mediocre commercial typography present on every wall and kiosk. The only thing that could make a meaningful impact would have to be elegant, colorful, and direct – capable of arresting the eye and transmitting a message in the most hostile and cluttered of environments.

A few American companies had devised advertisements that did just this. Huge designs, as large as thirteen feet across, were cut in wood and printed in cheerful colors to advertise traveling acrobats and circuses. Sometimes the posters bore the name of the troupe and needed to have only the time and place of performance added by a local impresario; other stock posters were provided for magicians or tumblers in general, and were provided with a personal identity by the performer who purchased them from the printer. One of the largest of these woodcut posters to survive (page 13) is also one of the earliest dated examples, having been deposited for copyright in 1856. It is impossible to say why this technique was not applied more generally to outdoor advertising; the fact remains that most other posters of the period are far smaller, and were ordinarily printed by black-and-white lithography.[2]

Woodcut posters accompanied groups of popular American performers to England, in the 1850's and 1860's, and must have been tremendously noticeable next to the dull broadsheets and handbills that provided the Englishman with his ordinary street literature. We know, at any rate, that they were noticed by a temporary resident, the young French lithographer Jules Chéret, who had come to England to become acquainted with advancements in the art of color lithography on that side of the Channel.[3]

Obviously color lithography was not essential to the production of pictorial

Fred Walker (English, 1840–1875).
The Woman in White. 1871.
Wood engraving, 7½ x 4⅜ inches.
Victoria and Albert Museum, London.

Edouard Manet (French, 1832–1883).
Champfleury—Les Chats. 1868.
Lithograph, 21⅝ x 17½ inches.
Bibliothèque des Arts Décoratifs, Paris.

Tony Johannot (French, 1803–1852).
Don Quichotte illustré. 1845.
Lithograph, 26¾ x 20½ inches.
Library of Congress, Washington, D.C.

Joseph W. Morse (American).
Five Celebrated Clowns. 1856.
Woodcut, 103 x 135 inches.
Library of Congress, Washington, D.C.

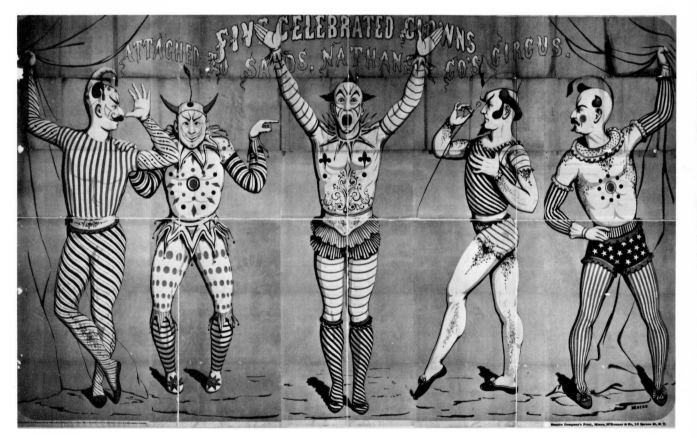

posters, but because there were fewer mechanical steps between the original design and the printed sheet, and because of the comparative freedom of designing for lithography, this process was viewed with favor by the producers of commercial printing. Color lithography had been envisioned by the inventor of the process himself, Alois Senefelder, at a very early date;[4] but, although small editions could be created by the painstaking overprinting of colors in perfect registration, a practical system of mass-produced, full-color lithography was not so easy to achieve. By the time of the Crystal Palace exhibition in 1851 it was clear that British printers had a commanding lead in this field. Several printers in France and Germany showed creditable work, but none had as long experience or as brilliant results as George Baxter, Charles Knight, or Owen Jones.[5] It was natural, therefore, that a printer who wished to perfect his knowledge of color printing should go to England, as Chéret did.

When he returned to France, to start his career again, Chéret carried with him not only the technical knowledge he had gained but also the memory of the American circus posters he had seen. In 1869 he produced his own first poster: a bright, informal, lively advertisement for Lydia Thompson's performance in *Faust* (page 14). It was an immediate success, and by common consent marks the beginning of the modern illustrated poster.[6]

Chéret's debt to the American circus poster is clearly expressed in another of his early designs, *Les Girard* (page 25), in which the lithe curves of the dancers animate the whole composition and intertwine amusingly with the lettering. The letters themselves seem to have caught something of the nervous energy of the Girards, and have become inseparable from the rest of the design. Chéret utilized the freedom of the lithographic process admirably, drawing letters that were totally in keeping with the pictorial forms of his posters. In letterpress printing there was a temptation to use type that had been designed for other purposes; in lithography (at least until the perfection of photographic platemaking) everything had to be drawn. To be sure, most lithographers drew letters that resembled type as closely as possible, but this was nothing more than the conservatism of the unimaginative commercial printer.

Soon Chéret had abandoned the fluid silhouette and had begun to evolve the jagged forms (page 25) that characterize his best known posters. Reflecting the verve and theatrical assurance of the eighteenth-century artists he admired, such as Tiepolo, his colors became more festive, lighter; he experimented with stippled and spattered tones, and became expert in the employment of transparent inks to achieve his elegant and subtly mixed colors. It was not long before the up-to-date French entertainer or businessman felt compelled to commission posters of a quality that would compare favorably with Chéret's work, by now such an important part of the Parisian scene. Interest in the poster as

an art was awakened. In 1884, Ernest Maindron wrote the first serious history of the poster[7] – the forerunner of his elaborate books on French and foreign posters of the 1890's; in 1888, the first exhibition of posters ever to be held took place in Paris.[8]

In 1889 a champagne bottler in Reims commissioned a young but promising painter, Pierre Bonnard, to design a poster worthy to be shown next to a Chéret.[9] *France-Champagne* (page 27) was the result, and it brought Bonnard to the attention of Henri de Toulouse-Lautrec. After their meeting (and in all likelihood as a result of it) Lautrec himself determined to try his hand at poster design. Thus it was that twenty years after the birth of the modern, color-lithographed poster, the attention of painters was brought to bear on the medium; to the fantastic productivity and brilliance of Chéret was added the incredibly subtle yet potent art of Bonnard and Lautrec, and the interest in posters turned into a mania.

The work of Bonnard is strikingly different from that of Chéret, although there are enough similarities in conception to confirm the debt owed by the younger artist. In *France-Champagne* the nervous, broken outline, the restricted color scheme, and the freely drawn lettering all seem to emerge from the work of Chéret, but they are transformed. In particular, the calligraphic fluency of Bonnard's heavy outline, and the unusual high viewpoint from which the figure is seen, mark his conception as original.

In his later posters Bonnard explored a variety of styles. His *Salon des Cent* (page 27) suggests more than a casual affinity with Lautrec in the bold simplicity of the figure, the telling use of blank space, and the flat pattern on the garment of the figure. By contrast, *La Revue Blanche* (page 26) is complex and active, with the figure pushed forward through the artful ambiguity of space and outline. It is striking to see how Bonnard's use of lettering reinforces the design of these posters. In *France-Champagne* only the lettering at the top enjoys this relationship; one assumes that the printer added the characterless text at the bottom, in conflict with the rest of the design. The spare, linear letters of *Salon des Cent* and the attenuated letters used in *La Revue Blanche* show how completely integrated the design could be if left to Bonnard himself. Bonnard and another friend, Edouard Vuillard, also designed theater programs and book covers, and with Chéret can share the distinction of departing from the traditional dull paper binding in France.

Lautrec has come to be regarded as a paragon of poster designers, even though he was not the first or the most prolific practitioner of the art. The images he created are indelibly striking and memorable: Chéret designed more than 1200 posters, yet it is difficult to recall the details of many of them, while Lautrec designed only 32 – but most of them are difficult to forget, once seen.

Jules Chéret (French, 1836–1932).
Faust! Lydia Thompson. 1869.
Lithograph.

Henri de Toulouse-Lautrec (French,
1864–1901).
Yvette Guilbert. 1894.
Lithograph, 9½ x 7½ inches.
The Metropolitan Museum of Art,
New York (Harris Brisbane Dick Fund,
1923).

Like Bonnard, Lautrec started using the technique of color lithography when he designed his first poster in 1891, but almost at once he proved himself a master of the art. He was able to compose simply, draw freely, letter boldly, and urge rich, dark colors out of the stone. Neither Lautrec nor the other pioneers relied on other craftsmen to render their designs in color lithography. Each color had to be evolved separately, with a sense of how the inks would mix and how the different areas would register when printed from separate stones.

There were several ways of working, the most common of which was to make a drawing as a study or guide (Lautrec commonly did this with oil paint on paper), and then to draw the most telling portion of the design onto the first stone – the one, say, to be printed in black. Proofs from this stone were then used as a guide for those to be printed in other colors; the artist had to be sure that each portion of his design would relate properly to the other colors when printed, since the printing was done in a commercial shop from the proofs approved by the artist. In our own century, photographic means are often used to transfer drawings onto lithographic printing surfaces, or else skilled craftsmen copy the artist's design and make the color separations required. But demanding as it was to master the art of color lithography, Lautrec and his contemporaries probably sensed that only in this way could they retain the brilliance and spontaneity they expected in their finished work.

Lautrec's poster Divan Japonais (page 28) contains most of the ingredients of his art, and repays close examination. In bold silhouette at the center is a woman extending her fan to the left; inclining towards her, at the right, a gentleman with a noble beard touches his cane appreciatively to his lips; while in the background – above an orchestra – the body (but not the head) of a singer occupies the upper left of the composition. The swinging curves of the chair, the necks of the bass viols, the contours of the bodies, and the black gloves of the singer, all set up a complex series of echoes and relationships. Essentially, only four flat tones are used, but they are employed so artfully that the image is powerful, memorable, and witty. Moreover, although the impact of the poster is immediate, one does not tire of seeing it repeatedly; this is important, when such a piece of advertising is likely to be posted all over town, and often repeated several times in one location.

Of course, none of these considerations would have troubled the Parisian public when Divan Japonais first went on the walls. They would have recognized at once that Jane Avril was in the audience (on a busman's holiday), listening to Yvette Guilbert. This instant recognition in itself was largely a result of Lautrec's work as a poster artist, for he (and his French colleagues) had discovered how to transplant from the art of caricature a strong sense of personality and individual physiognomy through the sparing use of line and gesture. A

comparison of Lautrec's posters in which Yvette Guilbert and Jane Avril are portrayed makes this point forcibly. Through the combination of her prominent chin and yellow hair, Jane Avril emerges as a woman of almost aristocratic bearing; Yvette Guilbert is instantly characterized by black gloves and long neck. Other poster designers, such as Chéret, Henri Dumont, and Théophile-Alexandre Steinlen (pages 30–31), reinforced this image, but without the wit and animation that give such impact to Lautrec's work. The entertainers themselves were often reluctant to accept Lautrec's biting imagery – Yvette Guilbert is said to have preferred Steinlen's poster to a design submitted by Lautrec (page 14) – but it is through Lautrec's posters that the character of these stars of the cafés-concerts emerges indelibly.

Steinlen was nonetheless a particularly important figure in the new poster art. He had come to Paris in 1878 from his native Switzerland, and had become a well known illustrator. His motifs often came from the raffish world of the cafés and boulevards. Perhaps because his work was less daring than Lautrec's it was more popular. When, in the 1890's, his posters gained wide circulation they inspired young artists in Belgium and in the United States to use color lithography in the design of posters, and to work in bold outlines of black, olive green, and orange-red.

Bonnard and Lautrec were not merely followers of Chéret. They were serious painters, alert to the lessons of other adventurous French artists in a time of considerable artistic ferment, and anxious to learn the lessons of color and composition to be found in such far-off sources as the Japanese woodcut. But most significant, they carried the most subtle lessons of the avant-garde artist to a broad audience, which otherwise remained unimpressed with the new painting. The poster craze that then came into being is testimony to this.[10]

Books, magazines, poster shops, all sprang into existence to satisfy the demand. New posters were ripped from the walls, until the publishers had enough wit to print overruns (which also made a profitable sideline for the printers).

Perhaps the most striking recognition of the new art of the poster was that by artists themselves. The poster craze became international; beginning in 1891 posters were exhibited alongside paintings[11] and criticized with equal seriousness. New artists of talent entered the field of poster design, and were decently rewarded for their efforts. Most significant of all, the poster was a crucial factor in establishing the link between new work in painting and new thinking in the decorative arts, a link that underlay the development of Art Nouveau, which in turn led directly to the stylistic revolution of early twentieth-century German, Dutch, and Austrian designers. That revolution will occupy us later; for now, let us turn to a consideration of Art Nouveau in all its strange variety.

William Morris (English, 1834–1896).
Border decoration and text for The
History of Godefrey of Boloyne. 1893.
Printed by the Kelmscott Press.

Aubrey Beardsley (English,
1872–1898).
A Comedy of Sighs! 1894.
Lithography and letterpress,
30 x 20 inches.
Acquired by exchange.

James McNeill Whistler (American,
1834–1903).
Title page for The Gentle Art of
Making Enemies. 1893.

If the great strength of Chéret, Bonnard, and Toulouse-Lautrec was in their ability to bring a sense of color and *joie-de-vivre* to the poster, the great accomplishment of Art Nouveau was that it explored other emotional realms that could be evoked in graphic terms.

Art Nouveau, contrary to widely held opinion, is not a single style but a series of related styles,[12] having in common a preference for colors that are admixtures – not primaries – and for curves that are serpentine, not arcs. The changing, the elusive, and the transitory seem to have held a fascination for Art Nouveau artists, and they often sought beauty in exotic echoes of Eastern art, or in such insubstantial moods as languor, yearning, or despair. Essentially, Art Nouveau was an anti-historical, linear, symbolist attempt to bring to all the arts a unity of design, or – at least – to bring a unity of approach to the solution of design problems.

Such artists as Chéret and Lautrec did not trouble to theorize about their work, or attempt to relate it to the other visual arts. In contrast, the Art Nouveau artist was a theorist *par excellence,* and was deeply concerned about the relationship of his work to the entire visual context within which life was lived. His work was bound up in a conscious reassessment of the decorative arts that culminated fifty years of exploration.

Beginning with the great Crystal Palace exposition of 1851, British artists began to reconsider the relationship between the "fine arts" and industrial design, and to try to discover appropriate principles of design for all the arts and crafts.

A similar effort took place in France about the same time, under the impetus of such designers and theorists as Viollet-le-Duc, but the British based their efforts on a more solid foundation and soon came to assume a position of leadership. Following the Crystal Palace show, and encouraged by the official sanction of Prince Albert, schools of the arts and crafts were instituted in England and Scotland and on the Continent. Carlyle and Ruskin had pointed to the increasing alienation of the laboring classes since the Industrial Revolution, and suggested that British society lacked the creative force essential to a healthy culture. This led a group of young artists to search for ways in which the toil of labor could be turned to creative energy, and the production of useful objects could become a positive and life-enhancing force.

In the typographic arts, one result was the private-press movement, led by William Morris and Emery Walker from 1888. The focusing of activity in this way, and the production of magnificently printed books, has tended to obscure the fact that there were others – Whistler among them – who also experimented with typography in the 1880's (page 17). The Morris group looked to the fifteenth century for inspiration, partly because they felt that the artist had a particularly effective role in society at that time, and partly because they felt that the new

THE GENTLE ART
of
MAKING ENEMIES
AS PLEASINGLY EXEMPLIFIED
IN MANY INSTANCES, WHEREIN THE SERIOUS ONES
OF THIS EARTH, CAREFULLY EXASPERATED, HAVE
BEEN PRETTILY SPURRED ON TO UNSEEMLINESS
AND INDISCRETION, WHILE OVERCOME BY AN
UNDUE SENSE OF RIGHT

LONDON MCMLIII
WILLIAM HEINEMANN LTD.

art of printing then had its finest expression. Moreover, Whistler, Charles Ricketts, and a few other artists became aware of the expressive possibilities of Japanese art and recognized the emotional power of such artists as Botticelli and William Blake. All this activity had the effect of making the typographic arts a legitimate field of endeavor for the "fine" artist, and of placing before the world the gulf between excellent design and the existing decorative arts.

This also had a marked impact on artists and teachers outside England, through international exhibitions and the publication of magazines devoted to the arts and crafts. In 1891, for example, the book illustrations of Walter Crane were shown at the Salon des XX in Brussels, alongside the paintings of Belgian and French independent artists. As has already been remarked, the posters of Chéret were also included in this invitational exhibition, suggesting yet another ingredient in the development of Art Nouveau. As it happened, one of the young Belgian artists in the 1891 exhibition was Henry van de Velde,[13] who had already begun to consider turning from painting to the design of useful objects. With the example of Walter Crane and Chéret before him, van de Velde in 1892 devoted himself to typographic design in earnest, and consciously worked to evolve a style that would owe nothing to the art of the past.

The new approach, which embraced every aspect of the arts and crafts, is what we have come to call Art Nouveau. Philosophy, craftsmanship, literature, and technology came together to create a brilliant, if sometimes disturbing, environment. National and personal characteristics tended to be submerged in the new style, along with the "debris" of history, in a search for a new grammar of form. By 1895, the style had a name – or, more precisely, a series of names, ranging from the affectionate (Yachting Style) to the derogatory (*Bandwurmstil,* or "tapeworm style") – and a series of central locations and periodicals. By 1905 it had deteriorated into a meaningless series of mannerisms, and its creators had turned to other modes of expression.

During its brief brilliant period of vitality, however, Art Nouveau made several essential contributions to the graphic art of the twentieth century. For the first time, the explicit emotional qualities of letter forms were recognized. At the same time that artists were learning of the evocative potentialities of forms and colors in themselves (as apart from their function in representing objects), they learned that the shapes and forms of letters could be manipulated in the same way and could become an inextricable part of a consistent design.

In general, the intent of the Art Nouveau artist was to symbolize, not to represent. Following French and British writers, a number of artists (such as Maurice Denis) advocated the evocation of feeling through allusion, or through the evocative qualities inherent in line, form, and color. Although there seems to be a direct link between much of the work of Art Nouveau and the posters of Chéret and

Lautrec, in one sense at least they are at cross purposes: whatever else Lautrec may have been, he was not allusive or symbolic in his work. Art Nouveau posters thus also depart sharply from the traditional advertising of the 1870's and 1880's, which was absolutely literal in the representation of products and of the consumers using them.

Since the formal elements of the visual arts had become endowed with a primary communicative function, the Art Nouveau designer was impelled to emphasize the flat pattern of his graphic design as never before. White space came to be used as a design element: there was an ambiguity in the relationship between the shapes that were actually drawn and the areas between them, which was in keeping with the ambiguity of the motifs themselves.

To support the work that was being done, new type faces were designed in the mid-1890's, which differed from the types of the private-press movement in that they did not spring from the classic type faces of the fifteenth century but rather from the lettering of the modern artist. This was just a part of a sweeping re-examination of materials and forms. New papers, new inks, and such newly perfected printing techniques as photoengraving were investigated; traditional practices of the past were discarded, when necessary, and fresh working methods were evolved.

Although the new style spread across the world with unprecedented speed, there were several centers in which it was practiced with the greatest vigor and creativity. Brussels, where the Groupe des XX was based, seems to have been a particularly fertile ground for the growth of the graphic arts. We have already mentioned the impact of Walter Crane and his fellow British arts-and-crafts designers on Henry van de Velde. The latter also found much to admire in the work of William Morris (especially in his social theories), so that when he turned to graphic design it was with the ideas of such men in mind.

Unlike Morris and the private-press artists, van de Velde worked within the context of commercial printing. He designed illustrations and ornament to be reproduced by photomechanical techniques (in contrast to the original woodcuts with which the private-press designers worked), and he sought industrial patrons who would be understanding even if they might not be glamorous. In 1897, after his work had been shown in Dresden – another of the important centers of the movement – van de Velde came to the attention of a number of German patrons, among them the proprietors of Insel-Verlag and the food-processing firm of Tropon. For the publisher, he developed further the simple book typography style he had begun in Belgium, but for Tropon he effectively initiated a new art: the total industrial graphic design (page 39). Posters, trademarks, packages, all utilized a group of related nonobjective designs and striking color combinations that gave Tropon products a memorable identity.

Otto Eckmann (German, 1865–1902).
Title page for Die Woche. 1899.

The emergence of these non-representational motifs has never been sufficiently studied. Others have traced a relationship between the devices used by Mackmurdo and Whistler, and van de Velde's early typographic ornaments (from which the Tropon designs derive),[14] but there were other currents in the air as well. Georges Auriol, Otto Eckmann, and Rudolph von Larisch, among others, investigated the expressive possibilities of the monogram in the nineties, deriving increasingly abstract forms out of the combination of letters (page 18). At the same time, Maurice Denis in France, Lucien Pissarro and Charles Ricketts in England, and Josef Hoffman in Austria were talking and writing about the necessity to create nonobjective ornament as a symbolic accompaniment to book typography. It is unlikely that all this was related, but something was in the air, and Art Nouveau was the collective result.

I have considered van de Velde's work at some length because of his later importance, but also because in some respects it is typical of the finest designing of the period. There were nonetheless many other artists in Belgium, and elsewhere, whose work also merits attention. Jan Toorop's renowned salad-oil posters (page 39) are just as personal and inventive as van de Velde's but in an entirely different vein. Toorop's designs are printed in remarkable soft colors, giving the surface a flat, glowing effect. Every area is animated with an undulating, repeated linear motif, and the figures entrapped in the surrounding activity are elegant, elongated, and immobile. The Dutch Toorop was one of the "Anglophile Vingtistes" (to borrow Bruce Laughton's phrase[15]), who were instrumental in getting the work of Crane, Arthur H. Mackmurdo, Herbert Horne, and Aubrey Beardsley to be shown in Belgium; and it is interesting to see how the English arts-and-crafts work is transformed by Toorop and his colleagues. More than a trace of Beardsley appears in their posters, but so altered in color and composition as to become entirely new.

Aubrey Beardsley himself worked primarily in black and white, and combined a thin, precisely limited line with unbroken areas of black or with tiny dotted motifs (page 16). The most striking thing about Beardsley's work, and the source of its immediate fame, is the intense, erotic (or better, narcissistic) atmosphere it exudes. Once the shock of recognition passes, it can be seen that Beardsley was an incredibly assured draughtsman and a perversely inventive designer. In his posters and book illustrations, he was able to compose in odd-shaped areas, and even seems to have preferred doing so; one is often confronted with such a barrier as the edge of a piece of furniture or the head of a figure at the margin of the composition (page 36).

From its debut in 1892, in the form of illustrations for Morte d'Arthur strongly influenced by the Kelmscott Press designs of William Morris, Beardsley's work never left the public eye, even with his premature death in 1898. His 1894 illustrations for Oscar Wilde's Salomé revealed a style that was utterly personal and quite without precedent in British art. M. H. Spielmann in 1895 epitomized the sophisticated reaction to Beardsley's work in what is surely one of the longest sentences in art criticism: "Meanwhile Mr. Aubrey Beardsley had appeared on the artistic horizon – a draughtsman of weird and singular power, who, after importing in his art elements so suggestively opposite as his distorted echoes of Chinese or Annamite execution and Rossettian feeling, seen with a squinting eye, imagined with a mephistophelian brain, and executed with a vampire hand, showed a deep natural instinct for the beauty of line, for the balance of chiaroscuro, and for decorative effect."[16]

The names of several other British designers have already been mentioned, in connection with the development of early Art Nouveau work in Belgium, but they were not among the most important poster designers in the British Isles. Walter Crane, for example, although he produced a few posters, held the art in contempt. In The Modern Poster he is quoted as saying, "I fear that there is something essentially vulgar about the idea of the poster unless it is limited to simple announcements or directions, or becomes a species of heraldry or sign painting.... The very fact of the necessity of shouting loud, and the association with vulgar commercial puffing, are against the artist and so much dead weight."[17] Unfortunately this attitude of withdrawal was typical of much of the arts-and-crafts movement, even though the work of its participants was an inspiration to others who were not so squeamish about reforming the vulgar commercial world. It was left to these others to transform the lessons of the arts-and-crafts movement into significant work for commercial purposes, intended for machine production. In large part, this transformation is what Art Nouveau accomplished, in addition to its superb achievements in the handicrafts themselves.

Towards the end of the decade in England, such excellent posters as those of Dudley Hardy and A.A. Turbayne were being produced (pages 36, 37), but the most remarkable work on that side of the Channel came from Scotland. In Glasgow the young architect Charles Rennie Mackintosh, along with two or three artists in his circle, designed a series of extraordinary posters (pages 19, 37) that created an immediate stir abroad through publication in books and magazines. They are quite different from any of the work we have been considering: the pulsing, serpentine line of Continental Art Nouveau is entirely absent; in its place are nearly rectilinear forms, highly stylized (and almost depersonalized) figures, and elaborate intertwinings of lines and planes both in the pictorial and textual elements. Their posters are incredibly long rectangles, with proportions attentuated to bony spareness.

Nothing could be farther from the boldly drawn, spattered, lively designs of

Frances Macdonald (Scottish,
1874–1921),
Margaret Macdonald (Scottish,
1865–1933), and
Herbert McNair (Scottish, 1864–?).
The Glasgow Institute of the Fine Arts.
c. 1894.
Lithograph, 93⅛ x 39⅞ inches.
Acquired by exchange.

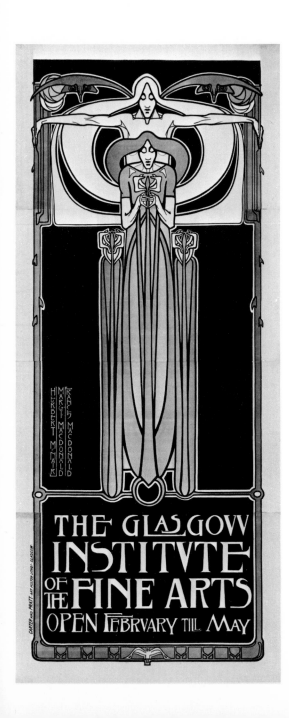

Lautrec than the complex posters of Mackintosh and the Macdonald sisters. As in the Tropon designs of van de Velde, there is an ambiguity in the interplay of drawn line and empty space, but here it is carried much farther. It is impossible to discern just what the relationship is between figure and border; the parts change function through space, just as the cat's tail in Dumont's poster becomes the dress of Yvette Guilbert; but there is much more subtlety to the Scottish posters than in any of the French work at the time.

It seems likely that some of the formal ideas of the Glasgow poster artists may have resulted from their experience with metalwork and architecture. This was certainly a characteristic of the mature Art Nouveau, in which the design of all objects was related as closely as possible. Adolphe Crespin's monumental poster for the architect Paul Hankar (page 38) places the conventionally drawn figure against a remarkable background of tiles, and frames him in the tools of his trade. Even more extraordinary is the unique *Castel Béranger* poster (page 36) designed by the architect Hector Guimard, in which letter forms – manifestly related to his big three-dimensional designs – are freely and handsomely composed.

In Germany and Austria, however, more direct echoes of the work of Mackintosh and the Macdonalds are found, in the work of artists associated with the several anti-academic architecture and crafts schools. The long rectangles and assertively flat compositions of Peter Behrens, Alfred Roller, Koloman Moser, and J.M. Olbrich are all noteworthy in this respect. The Austrians, in particular, excelled in the use of bold, over-all patterns – often combining several motifs from different areas into posters that seem almost Oriental in character. Undoubtedly, there is a relationship between the later mosaic and painted work of Gustav Klimt, and the posters of Roller, Moser (page 42), and Olbrich.

Just as van de Velde devoted much of his time to the design of books and printed ephemera, so the German and Austrian anti-academic artists were much concerned with typographic design. Peter Behrens designed not only a factory for the Allgemeine Elektrizitäts Gesellschaft (the German General Electric firm), but also produced letterheads, pamphlets, and magazine advertisements for the company. Moreover, Behrens, Moser, and Olbrich were among the most inventive of book designers in their countries, which were just emerging from a long fallow period in the graphic arts.

France in the 1890's was also the scene of a diverse and creative group of poster designers, following the lead of Chéret, Bonnard, and Lautrec. Jacques Villon's poster for Le Grillon (page 32) would assure him a spot in any history of the graphic arts, even if he were not otherwise a powerful figure in the history of modern painting. Eugène Grasset, Steinlen, and a score of others carried on this lively art and created enduring designs. It would not do to leave

Eugène Grasset (French, 1841–1917).
The January Century. 1894.
Lithograph, 28 x 20 inches.
Library of Congress, Washington, D.C.

Lucian Bernhard (German, born
1883).
Buy German Savings Bonds. c. 1920.
Lithograph, 27½ x 39½ inches.
Library of Congress, Washington, D.C.

France without mentioning the extraordinary work of Alphonse Mucha, who came to Paris to study in 1890 and burst into fame in 1894 with his renowned posters for Sarah Bernhardt (page 33). Mucha created a remarkably vivid effect by the contrast between flat, complex decorative motifs and softened, modeled elements within the figures. The formal weavings of his patterns resemble, perhaps coincidentally, the decorative panels of the architect Louis Sullivan; Mucha punctured these shapes so that the colors of his backgrounds came through, establishing the effect of an overlay of several spatial planes. Something similar occurs in Moser's poster for *Frommes Kalender* (page 42), and indeed Mucha's style seems to have been quickly appreciated by his fellow eastern Europeans.

The poster craze was carried into the United States at a relatively early date. In 1889 Grasset was commissioned to do a cover for *Harper's Bazaar* and a poster for *Harper's Magazine;* a few years later he designed posters for the *Century* (page 20). Throughout the nineties there was much activity along these lines by American artists and publishers. Lautrec and Beardsley became familiar to readers of *The Chap Book* (for which Lautrec was commissioned to do a poster), and such journals as *The Studio* and *The Poster* seem to have enjoyed a wide circulation in this country.

Several American poster artists of accomplishment emerged in the 1890's. The young illustrator Will Bradley, working in the manner of Beardsley, Turbayne, and the Belgian artists whose work was reproduced in the journals, transformed their styles into exceptionally bold and successful designs that were usually printed by photomechanical processes (page 40). Edward Penfield's work (page 41), on the other hand, is far more in the spirit of Lautrec, Bonnard, or Steinlen.[18] He strove to maintain the feeling of the original lithograph in his posters, which share with Lautrec's the use of large open areas, unusual viewpoints, and warm, varied colors. American designers had a strong sense of pattern and compositional solidity, so their work transcends the merely routine adaptation of current European styles; dozens of artists could be added to this short list, such as Louis J. Rhead, Ethel Reed, Frank Hazenplug (page 42), and Will Carqueville, all of whom enjoyed considerable success.

One graphic artist of this period in the United States went on to become an important painter – John Sloan (page 41). In reminiscences recently published by his widow,[19] Sloan tells how he first became aware of the potentialities of illustration through contact with Walter Crane, and how his "poster style" was formed partly as a result of his excitement over the Beardsley drawings reproduced in *The Yellow Book,* which he was able to buy in Philadelphia in the nineties. As his style developed, Sloan recalled, he cared less for the bizarre aspects of Beardsley's art than for the posters of Steinlen. This account is not

only revealing about the work of Sloan; it also indicates how rapidly and easily new design in printing spread from one country to another, and how amenable artists were to this art that had so much vitality and power.

I have mentioned a number of intellectual and stylistic contributions of Art Nouveau to the twentieth century. Perhaps one more point should be made: artistic nationalism largely ceased to matter in the face of the easy transmission of new work across political borders. Internationalism in the visual arts, so taken for granted today, appears to date from the 1890's, and, since no artifact was more easily transported than the printed book or poster, graphic design was one of the main carriers of the new style.

By 1905 most of the innovators had abandoned Art Nouveau for other styles and other modes of expression. Van de Velde settled in Weimar, where he organized a system of education for artists and craftsmen that foreshadowed the famous Bauhaus, to be founded there some fifteen years later. Peter Behrens entered architectural practice, but inculcated such a strong sense of design exploration in his young students and associates that he also can be called one of the Bauhaus forefathers. In the Netherlands, a similar line of formal exploration was initiated, leading to a remarkable burst of creative endeavor in the 1920's. In the meantime, however, several undercurrents of the graphic arts in the 1890's came to the surface after the turn of the century; before turning to the Bauhaus and its accomplishments, let us examine the powerful art of German and Austrian expressionism as it was manifested in the posters of the decade or so before World War I.

After 1900, when poster design in France and England had died down somewhat, German artists who turned to the graphic arts did so with a vigor and productivity that seems almost incredible. The impact of both the arts-and-crafts movement and Art Nouveau on Germany had been considerable. A thoroughgoing reassessment of art style and art education was under way. The education adviser Hermann Muthesius and Harry Graf Kessler (publisher, author and diplomat), among others, gave official and unofficial counsel, and brought some of the most interesting developments of other nations into Germany for its artists and teachers to see.

The typographic arts were not exempt from this reassessment and transformation. The traditional *Fraktur,* or blackletter type, was being replaced by roman types in the most advanced circles, and as a result the art of letter design underwent a renaissance in Germany at the turn of the century. Following the example of Edward Johnston in England, craftsmen like Rudolph Koch became master calligraphers; and Walter Tiemann, E. R. Weiss, and a score of other talented designers turned their attention to letter design and typography around the turn of the century.

It was only natural that this new vitality in the arts should have resulted in some remarkable posters. The quality of work produced by talented German designers in the early decades of the twentieth century[20] may be exemplified by two of the most prolific and inventive, Lucian Bernhard and Ludwig Hohlwein.

In discussing their work, I should first mention two significant predecessors from the decade before. James Pryde and William Nicholson, a team of British artists who signed themselves the Beggarstaff Brothers, worked during the height of the Art Nouveau period, but their own style was very different. The Beggarstaffs – and Nicholson in particular – were masters of simplified form (page 44). Working in both woodcut and color lithography, they designed their figures in terms of utterly simple blocks of black and white, and added a subtle dimension through the use of a solid tone (often brown) out of which highlights were cut. This was an adaptation of the chiaroscuro woodcut, but while a traditional chiaroscuro artist worked in line over his tonal background, the Beggarstaff Brothers worked in simple masses – resorting to line only to delineate details and features. Nicholson, moreover, developed a fondness for blocky, squat letters related to the bold Clarendon types of the mid-nineteenth century, which were particularly suited to the heavy forms of his illustrations.

Around 1905 Lucian Bernhard began to design posters in Berlin, and almost at once found that he could work very effectively in this bold style. Bernhard was (and is, for he still lives in New York) a master lettering artist, and as he turned away from the standard *Fraktur* he began to experiment with a roman letter closely related to what he had seen in the work of the Beggarstaffs.[21]

Bernhard regularized this new letter style, and made it into an element of his design that had easily as much force as the pictorial design. There are several examples of his posters that contain no pictorial image at all (as is the case with certain designs of van de Velde and Guimard), yet which are full of vitality and have a powerful impact (page 21).

Ludwig Hohlwein began to design posters about the same time, and, like Gipkens, Klinger, and several other artists of the period, he followed along the same line Bernhard had chosen. Whether Hohlwein came to know the Beggarstaffs through Bernhard's work, or whether he arrived at his style independently, cannot be ascertained. In any case, he added a new dimension with his mastery of brilliant colors (which are further strengthened through being incorporated in the general brown tonality of his designs), and through the use of bold patterns, rendered with a complete disregard for the forms they were supposed to be covering. As a result, Hohlwein's posters (pages 43 – 45) seem assertively flat, and stress emphatically the two-dimensional character of the work.

An undercurrent of fantasy and eroticism distinguishes the Art Nouveau style from the more robust and matter-of-fact work of Bernhard and Hohlwein. Certain formal similarities suggest that the new generation in Germany had been to school during the Art Nouveau period, but with this masculine and assertive work a new spirit entered the graphic arts. Even the Beggarstaff Brothers did not infuse their work with the force and brilliance of their German followers: the figures do not seem to be larger than life, as do Hohlwein's and Bernhard's; the message is not stated with such firmness.

Hohlwein and Bernhard were graphic designers by profession. But one significant outgrowth of the activity at the turn of the century was the bringing together of painters and designers in a mutual effort to find a new style. It was firmly established that visual stimuli could be sources of strong emotion, and that the forms of art needed to depend very little on historical precedent. The designers were to go their own way, continuing their search for new forms, but in Germany and Austria the painters came to see that they had been given the tools for a new art of considerable power. Thus it was that in the first decade of the twentieth century there came into being a group of styles which have come to be known as expressionism, and thus also it happened that these expressionist artists naturally turned to the poster as one of their most compelling modes of communication.

The Expressionists

Ernst Ludwig Kirchner (German, 1880–1938).
KG Brüke in Galerie Arnold. 1905–07.
Color woodcut, 32¾ x 31⅞ inches.
Kaiser Wilhelm Museum, Krefeld.

"The greatest artist is the one who brings to life the most force, the most joy, the most vibration, the one from whom radiates for all the most ardor for life. The mission of the artist is to make us live a life more intense and to overcome the anemia of bourgeois life."[22] When Hermann Obrist wrote this in 1900, he meant to suggest that this was the direction in which the *Jugendstil* (or German Art Nouveau) artist was going, but it is significant that the force and ardor valued by Obrist were somewhat inhibited at the time, even though they seem more characteristic of German and Austrian Art Nouveau than of the style in other countries.

Around 1905, however, these very qualities began to be highly valued among artists in revolt against the established art styles of the schools and academies. First in Dresden and later in Berlin, the painters Ernst Ludwig Kirchner, Emil Nolde, Max Pechstein, Erich Heckel, and Karl Schmidt-Rottloff formed a group called *Die Brücke* ("The Bridge"), and reinforced by one another's work developed an art of intensity, directness, and power. In printmaking, which these men also practiced, they favored the direct media – woodcut, drypoint, and lithography – bringing to their prints the same slashing draughtsmanship and savage energy with which they endowed their painting.

For exhibitions, theatrical performances, and political campaigns, the artists of Die Brücke designed posters, and printed them by lithography and woodcut (page 22). In contrast to the polished, carefully executed designs of Behrens and Olbrich, their posters seem crude and unrefined. But Art Nouveau had become passé, and the new posters and graphic designs of Bernhard and Hohlwein were creating a different atmosphere for the graphic artist. Lovis Corinth, Käthe Kollwitz, and a number of artists not directly connected with Die Brücke also reflected the new directness in their work; and in Austria, Oskar Kokoschka began to produce monumental color lithograph posters (page 46) from 1907 onwards.

These designs were primarily concerned with gloomy emotions and powerful political convictions. Another expressionist group, Der Blaue Reiter ("The Blue Rider"), organized in Munich in 1911, worked in a more pleasant vein of lighter emotions and fantasy, but with the same sense of directness of execution, and vibration of color and form. Wassily Kandinsky was a founding member of the group, but his remarkable early poster for the Phalanx exhibition (page 47) hardly suggests his later work; instead, it seems to occupy a mid-point between the patterning of German Art Nouveau and the bold designs of Hohlwein. The precocious Viennese artist, Egon Schiele, also designed important posters (page 46), but explored a vein of feeling that is alternately neurotic and erotic. Like his colleagues in Germany, Schiele never lost the sense of direct drawing in his poster designs.

Perhaps it is this directness of approach that is the most significant contribution of expressionist artists to the poster. Their work in the medium began when the forces leading to World War I were first being felt, and they reacted boldly against the social outrages they saw around them. When the war finally came, they pointed the way to a new involvement of the artist in political affairs, and demonstrated the power of the graphic arts to affect opinion (pages 49–51). After the war, some of the expressionists (especially those in Munich) turned increasingly to abstraction and joined forces with the new art and craft school founded in Weimar by Behrens' student Walter Gropius. But the artists of Die Brücke seemed less anxious to turn away from their potent imagery, and through the 1920's up to the time of Hitler they provided a driving force to German art.

Fred G. Cooper (American, 1883–1962).
America's Tribute to Britain. 1918.
Woodcut, 29 x 20 inches.
Library of Congress, Washington, D.C.

With the coming of war and the subsequent political upheavals in Germany and Russia, the poster became a tool for propaganda to a degree unimagined by the nineteenth-century pioneers. A few earlier artists had suggested this potential power of the graphic arts. Steinlen, for example, working within the context of the poster style developed by Lautrec, was able to create moving and pointed posters directed towards the correction of social evils, and the coming of war brought forth some of his most powerful designs. The work of the German expressionists has already been mentioned in this connection.

In other countries, however, a curious hybrid was developed. The popular style of magazine illustration prevailing in the early 1900's in England and the United States was that of such artists as James Montgomery Flagg. Their work in watercolor and charcoal was derived from the bravura paintings of John Singer Sargent and Giovanni Boldini, and it was reproduced by newly improved photoengraving techniques in such a manner that every virtuoso brushstroke could be seen, even in the reproduction. It was felt that their popularity could be harnessed in the service of the war effort, and they were commissioned by both private and governmental agencies to design patriotic posters. Flagg's well-known *I Want You* (page 48) is a somewhat better than average result of this cross-breeding of magazine illustration and poster. Strangely enough, only a few people seemed to realize that work in this style could never approach the emotional power and punch of the German style of designing, which owed much less to illustration and fashionable painting. Erich Erler, Walter Lehmann, F.K. Engelhard, and Alfred Offner – not to mention Lucian Bernhard (page 49) – produced war posters of brooding power beside which the cute cartoons of Francisque Poulbot and the slick drawings of Flagg seem pallid.[23]

A few American artists seemed to understand the source of the power found in the designs of the other side. Fred G. Cooper, for example, learned much from Bernhard and Hohlwein – even to the use of lettering with stubby serifs – and produced several elegantly monumental posters (page 23) on behalf of the war effort. A few other artists came to posters during the war as a result of their work as printmakers, among them the lithographers Joseph Pennell (page 48), Frank Brangwyn, and Gerald Spencer Pryse, and they were also relatively successful.

After the war, when depression and revolution seized Europe, the work of the expressionist poster artists came into its fullest flower, and no posters are more poignant and compelling than those of Käthe Kollwitz. As the wife of a doctor, she had seen more than her share of suffering, and shortly after the turn of the century she began her notable cycles of prints dealing with death, malnutrition, and disease. She designed an occasional poster during the early 1900's, but her most emphatic statements came as her radical political beliefs

El Lissitzky (Eleazar Markovich;
Russian, 1890–1941).
Pages from The Story of Two
Squares. 1922.
Gift of Philip Johnson.

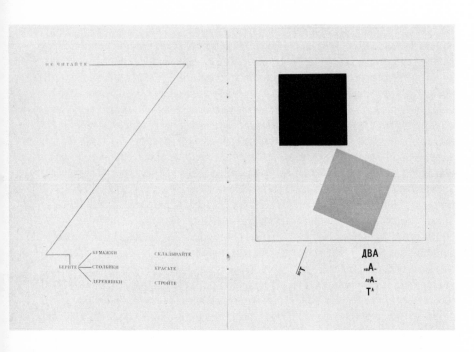

found expression in socialist politics after the war. Her posters are a direct transposition of her printmaking style, sometimes slightly enlarged but frequently printed directly from her lithographic image (page 50). Her message is as direct as her imagery: a dying mother is clutched by her many children, and the viewer is urged to support the orphans of Vienna.

Considering the powerful feelings involved, it is extraordinary that so few war and propaganda posters achieve the power and simplicity of which Kollwitz was master. Perhaps the use of styles thought to be popular with the general public, and the temptation to say too much and show too little, killed the majority of war posters. Even in the ferment of the Russian Revolution, most posters were little more than crude caricatures, or else academic painting reproduced for a political purpose.

In Russia, however, one new source of art took hold briefly, although it had but a short period of vitality in the new Soviet Union before it gave way to the banalities of people's art. As early as 1913, such artists as Vladimir Tatlin, Kasimir Malevich and El Lissitzky had begun an investigation of abstract form, aiming to reduce art to its essentials (page 24). Malevich and Lissitzky in particular strove to eliminate the distractions of brushwork and accident from their creations. They tended towards rectilinear forms and a monochromatic palette, although Lissitzky early experimented with pictorial elements from printed catalogues and magazines, introduced in a restrained way to enliven his compositions. The constructivists, as they came to be called, had considerable effect upon their contemporaries, but the atmosphere in the Soviet Union became increasingly inhospitable to such experimentation in art. In the mid-twenties Malevich and Lissitzky began to turn increasingly to their colleagues outside the Soviet Union; by the 1930's both had become exiles. Fortunately, in western Europe several new developments were under way that accorded perfectly with constructivism, and provided impetus for a new generation of graphic artists.

Jules Chéret (French, 1836–1932).

Les Girard. 1879.
Lithograph, 22⅝ x 17 inches.
Acquired by exchange.

Jules Chéret.

Palais de Glace Champs Elysées. 1893.
Lithograph, 48⅞ x 34¾ inches.
Acquired by exchange.

Pierre Bonnard (French, 1867–1947).

La Revue Blanche. 1894.
Lithograph, 31¾ x 24⅜ inches.
Purchase fund.

Henri de Toulouse-Lautrec (French, 1864–1901).

Jane Avril. 1899.
Lithograph, 22 x 14 inches.
Gift of Abby Aldrich Rockefeller.

Pierre Bonnard.

France-Champagne. 1891.
Lithograph, 30⅛ x 23 inches.
Purchase fund.

Pierre Bonnard.

Salon des Cent. 1896.
Lithograph, 22¾ x 15⅛ inches.
Purchase fund.

Henri de Toulouse-Lautrec.

Reine de Joie. 1892.
Lithograph, 59 x 38¾ inches.
Gift of Mr. and Mrs. Richard Rodgers.

Henri de Toulouse-Lautrec.

Divan Japonais. 1892.
Lithograph, 31⅞ x 24½ inches.
Purchase fund.

Henri de Toulouse-Lautrec.

Jane Avril. 1893.
Lithograph, 49⅝ x 36⅛ inches.
Gift of A. Conger Goodyear.

Henri de Toulouse-Lautrec.

Troupe de Mlle. Eglantine. 1896.
Lithograph, 24⅛ x 31¼ inches.
Gift of Abby Aldrich Rockefeller.

Henri de Toulouse-Lautrec.

Elles. 1896.
Lithograph, 20⅜ x 15¾ inches.
Gift of Abby Aldrich Rockefeller .

Henri Dumont (French, 1859 – ?).

Tous Les Soirs Aux Ambassadeurs Yvette Guilbert. c. 1900.
Lithograph, 82 x 32 inches.
Gift of Pierre Beres.

Jules Chéret.

Yvette Guilbert au Concert Parisien. 1891.
Lithograph, 48¾ x 34½ inches.
Gift of Lillian Nassau.

Théophile-Alexandre Steinlen (French, 1859–1923).

Yvette Guilbert. 1894.
Lithograph, 72½ x 31½ inches.
Anonymous gift.

Jacques Villon (French, 1875–1963).

Le Grillon. 1899.
Lithograph, 49 x 34⅝ inches.
Purchase fund.

Alphonse Mucha (Czech, 1860–1939; lived in France).

XXme Exposition du Salon des Cent. 1896.
Lithograph, 25¼ x 17 inches.
Gift of Ludwig Charell.

Alphonse Mucha

Médée Théâtre de la Renaissance Sarah Bernhardt. 1898.
Lithograph, 81¼ x 30 inches.
Gift of Joseph H. Heil.

Alphonse Mucha

Théâtre de la Renaissance Sarah Bernhardt La Samaritaine. 1897.
Lithograph, 70 x 24 inches.
Phyllis B. Lambert Fund.

Eugène Grasset (French, 1841–1917).

Salon des Cent Exposition E. Grasset. 1894.
Lithograph and letterpress, 23⅞ x 16¼ inches.
Gift of Ludwig Charell.

Manuel Orazi (French).

Théâtre de Loïe Fuller Exposition Universelle. 1900.
Lithograph, 78½ x 25¼ inches.
Gift of Joseph H. Heil.

Hector Guimard (French, 1867–1942).

Exposition Salon du Figaro le Castel Béranger. 1900.
Lithograph, 35 x 49¼ inches.
Gift of Lillian Nassau.

Aubrey Beardsley (British, 1872–1898).

Publisher. Children's Books. 1894.
Lithograph and letterpress, 30 x 20 inches.
Phyllis B. Lambert Fund.

A. A. Turbayne (British, 1866–?).

Macmillan's Illustrated Standard Novels. 1896.
Lithograph, 34⅝ x 22½ inches.
Acquired by exchange.

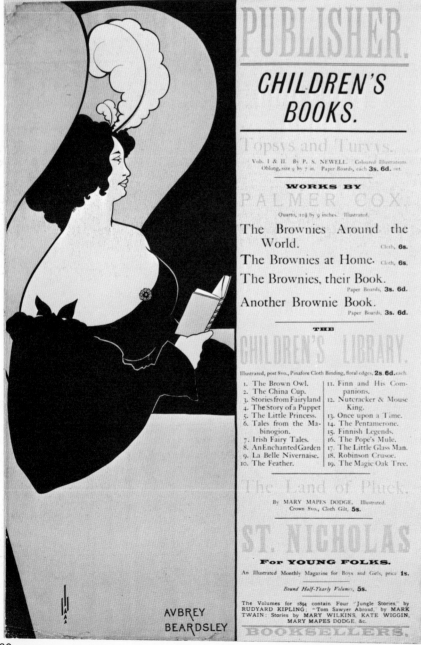

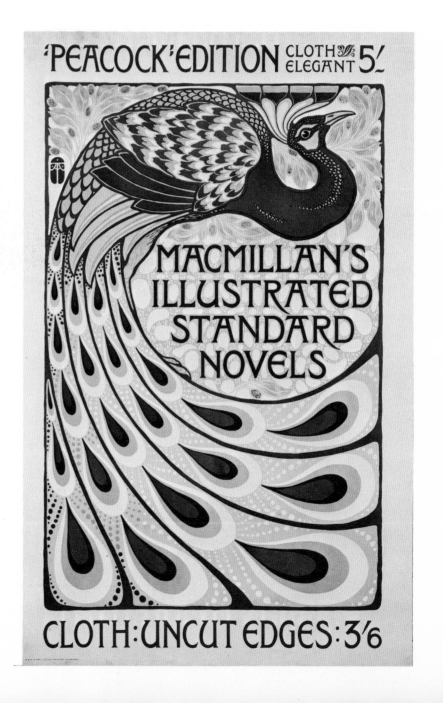

Dudley Hardy (British, 1886–1922).

A Gaiety Girl. c. 1895.
Lithograph, 89 x 39½ inches.
Promised gift of Mr. and Mrs. Paul Nassau.

Charles Rennie Mackintosh (Scottish, 1868–1928).

The Scottish Musical Review. 1896.
Lithograph, 97 x 39 inches.
Acquired by exchange.

Adolphe Crespin (Belgian, 1859–1944).

Paul Hankar Architecte. 1894.
Lithograph, 23 x 15½ inches.
Gift of Mr. and Mrs. Alan Kern.

Henri Meunier (Belgian, 1873–1922).

Pollet et Vittet Chocolaterie de Pepinster. c. 1896.
Lithograph, 19 x 26⅞ inches.
Gift of Joseph H. Heil.

Jan Toorop (Dutch, 1858–1928).

Delftsche Slaolie. 1895.
Lithograph, 36½ x 24⅛ inches.
Acquired by exchange.

Henry van de Velde (Belgian, 1863–1957).

Tropon l'Aliment le Plus Concentré (Tropon the Most Concentrated
Nourishment). 1899.
Offset facsimile of original lithograph, 31⅝ x 21⅜ inches.
Gift of Tropon-Werke.

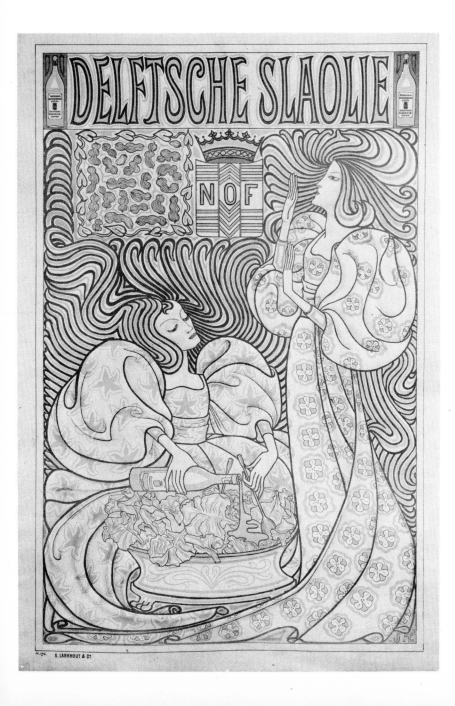

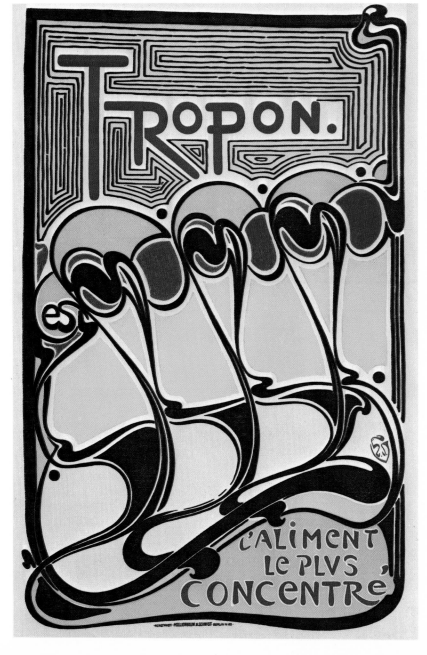

Will Bradley (American, 1868–1962).

The Inland Printer Christmas 1895.
Letterpress, 12½ x 8½ inches.
Gift of Joseph H. Heil.

Will Bradley

The Echo. c. 1895.
Lithograph, 23¾ x 15¾ inches.
Acquired by exchange.

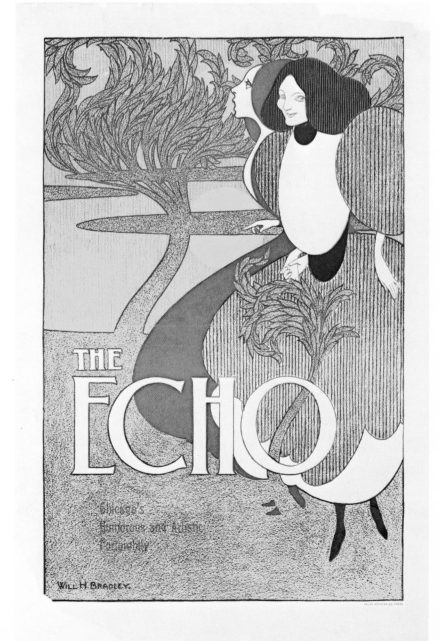

40

John Sloan (American, 1871–1951).

The Echo. 1895.
Lithograph, 18¾ x 8 inches.
Acquired by exchange.

Edward Penfield (American, 1866–1925).

Harper's March. 1897.
Lithograph, 14 x 19 inches.
Gift of Poster Originals.

Frank Hazenplug (American, born 1873 – ?).

The Chap-Book. 1895.
Lithograph, 21¼ x 13¾ inches.
Acquired by exchange.

Koloman Moser (Austrian, 1868 –1918).

Frommes Kalender. 1903.
Lithograph, 37½ x 24½ inches.
Anonymous gift.

Ludwig Hohlwein (German, 1874–1949).

Hermann Scherrer. Breechesmaker Sporting-Tailor. 1911.
Lithograph, 44¼ x 31½ inches.
Gift of Peter Muller-Munk.

Ludwig Hohlwein.

Confection Kehl. 1908.
Lithograph, 48½ x 36⅛ inches.
Gift of Peter Muller-Munk.

Beggarstaff Brothers:

James Pryde (Scottish, 1869–1941) and
William Nicholson (British, 1872–1904).

Rowntree's Elect Cocoa. 1895.
Lithograph, 38 x 28⅝ inches.
Gift of Mr. and Mrs. Arthur A. Cohen.

Ludwig Hohlwein.

Kunstgewerbehaus Gebrueder Wollweber. 1908.
Lithograph, 49½ x 35⅜ inches.
Gift of Peter Muller-Munk.

Ludwig Hohlwein.

Carl Stiller Jr. Schuhe. c. 1909.
Lithograph, 28⅜ x 37¾ inches.
Gift of Peter Muller-Munk.

Armand M. Rassenfosse (Belgian, 1862–1934).

Salon des Cent Exposition de Dessins Originaux et d'Estampes. 1896.
Lithograph, 22⅛ x 30¼ inches.
Gift of Ludwig Charell.

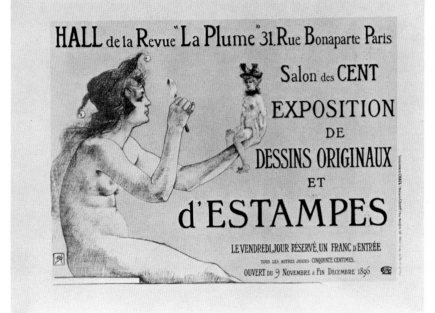

Oskar Kokoschka (British, born Austria, 1886).

Kokoschka Drama Komoedie. 1907.
Lithograph, 46½ x 30 inches.
Purchase fund.

Egon Schiele (Austrian, 1890–1918).

Shaw oder die Ironie. 1910.
Lithograph, 24½ x 14¼ inches.
Don Page Fund.

Wassily Kandinsky (Russian, 1866–1944; lived in Germany and France).

Phalanx 1. Ausstellung. 1901.
Lithograph, 19½ x 26⅜ inches.
Gift of Mme. Wassily Kandinsky.

James Montgomery Flagg (American, 1877–1960).

I Want You for U.S. Army. 1917.
Lithograph, 40¼ x 29½ inches.
Acquired by exchange.

Joseph Pennell (American, 1860–1926).

That Liberty Shall Not Perish from the Earth. c. 1917.
Lithograph, 40⅝ x 29¼ inches.
Gift of John D. Rockefeller III.

Lucian Bernhard (German, born 1883).

Das ist der Weg zum Frieden (That is the way to peace). 1914–1918.
Lithograph, 25¾ x 18¾ inches.
Gift of Peter Muller-Munk.

Jules-Abel Faivre (French, 1867–1945).

On les Aura! (We'll Win!) 1916.
Lithograph, 44½ x 31¼ inches.
Acquired by exchange.

49

Heinz Fuchs (German, born 1886).

Arbeiter Hunger Tod naht Streik zerstört Arbeit ernährt (Workers Hunger Death
Approach Strike Destroys Work Nourishes). 1919.
Lithograph, 29½ x 40¾ inches.
Gift of Peter Muller-Munk.

Käthe Kollwitz (German, 1867–1945).

Wien Stirbt! Rettet Seine Kinder! (Vienna Is Dying! Save Her Children). 1920.
Lithograph, 37 x 22 inches.
Anonymous gift.

Oskar Kokoschka.

Nieder mit dem Bolschewismus (Down With Bolshevism). 1919.
Lithograph, 26¼ x 39¼ inches.
Acquired by exchange.

Karl Michel (German, born 1885).

Faust. 1927.
Lithograph, 55½ x 36½ inches.
Gift of Universum-Film Aktiengesellschaft.

Schulz-Neudamm (German).

Metropolis. 1926.
Lithograph, 83 x 36½ inches.
Gift of Universum-Film Aktiengesellschaft.

Otto Stahl-Arpke (German, 1885 – 1943).

Das Cabinet des Dr. Caligari. 1919.
Lithograph, 27⅛ x 27 inches.
Gift of Universum-Film Aktiengesellschaft.

Unknown (German).

Der Golem. 1920.
Lithograph, 28½ x 37 inches.
Gift of Universum-Film Aktiengesellschaft.

Josef Albers (American, born
Germany, 1888).
Display alphabet. 1923.
Opaque glass, maximum height of
characters, 3⅛ inches.
Gift of the designer.

The war shattered many institutions in Germany, and as the country undertook
the rebuilding of its social and political structure it also re-examined its art. An
entirely new ingredient had entered the art of painting, having come from many
sources (including Art Nouveau and its aftermath) and taking many forms. This
was abstraction. The cubists in France had succeeded in breaking apart the
familiar canons of representation of objects, and Kandinsky had ceased to
represent objects in his dynamic paintings and prints. Non-representational art
was now a force with which the young artist had to reckon, and he was quite
willing to do so, since the basically non-representational crafts had been
elevated to equality with the other visual arts back at the turn of the century.
Van de Velde's typographic designs, for example, were often totally divorced
from the imitation of natural forms, and those poster designers who had used
lettering exclusively had proven that a compelling design did not require the
presence of a recognizable picture in order to communicate.

The commitment of artists to new design principles at the moment when new
institutions were required in Germany resulted in the foundation of a remarkable
school at Weimar, called the Bauhaus, which was dedicated to the training of a
new breed of artist: a man equally at home in architecture, industrial design,
stage design, typography, or painting, and committed to the discovery of the
basic principles of his art. Van de Velde had attempted something of this kind in
Weimar before the war, but personal and artistic jealousies, as well as political
problems, closed the school before the outbreak of war. In 1919 Walter Gropius,
who had been working with Peter Behrens, organized an institution that quickly
developed its own set of problems (which must have sounded familiar to
van de Velde as he watched it from afar). Nonetheless, the Bauhaus remained
for six years at Weimar, and then moved to Dessau, where it survived until the
early 1930's.

This is not the place to set down a history of the school, or to analyze its
teaching and accomplishments in detail. But it must be mentioned as the single
most influential force of its decade; it was an institution with which every
designer had to agree or fight. It was practically impossible, at least in Europe,
to ignore the Bauhaus altogether. Other centers were also involved in this
evolution, and employed similar principles. Schools and individual masters in
London, Amsterdam, Brussels, Berlin, and Leipzig (among many others) were
producing work of the highest quality. A graduate of the Leipzig Academy of
Book Design, Jan Tschichold (pages 69, 76, 105), in 1935 made one of the most
emphatic statements of the basis of the new typographic art:

"The connection between 'abstract' painting and the new typography does not
lie in the use of 'abstract' forms but in similarity of working methods. In both,
the artist must first make a scientific study of his available materials and then,

Walter Dexel (German, born 1890).
Advertisement for Gaskoks. c. 1926.
Letterpress.
Gift of Philip Johnson.

Johannes Itten (Germany, 1888–1967).
Greetings and Hail to the Hearts. 1924.
Lithograph, 14 x 9⅞ inches.
Gift of Samuel A. Berger.

El Lissitzky.
Program cover. 1919–20?
Letterpress.
Gift of Philip Johnson.

using contrast, forge them into an entity....The works of 'abstract' art are subtle creations of order out of simple, contrasting elements. Because this is exactly what typography is trying to do, it can derive stimulus and instruction from a study of such paintings, which communicate the visual forms of the modern word and are the best teachers of visual order.''[24]

Perhaps the most striking characteristic of the typography of the 1920's was its reliance on asymmetry (page 63). Actually this was nothing new; Whistler and George Bernard Shaw had used it in their widely circulated books. But the postwar designers on the Continent added a further ingredient: the use of ornament based entirely on the precise geometric forms of the rectangle and circle, and the almost exclusive use of a geometrically based sans-serif type. Designers worked with elements of their posters and booklet covers set at a 45-degree angle, or with lines of type running up and down at right angles to other lines in the text. In keeping with the interest in mechanical developments, photography was frequently used as an illustrative element (and more will be said about photography presently) adding contrast to the otherwise non-representational design units.

It should not be inferred from this that the work produced by the masters and apprentices of the Bauhaus was uniform in character. Quite the reverse is true. Walter Dexel in a recent statement[25] emphatically denies the existence of a ''Bauhaus style,'' and his own work suggests that this denial is true. As a young designer he designed splendidly asymmetrical announcements (page 56), built entirely from straight lines, circular forms, and colors in solid blocks. As his style developed he showed a predilection for the imaginative combination of typographic elements as decorative forms (pages 63, 64), to the exclusion of pictorial illustration. Herbert Bayer, one of the masters at the Bauhaus, often used photography in his compositions. His colleagues Lyonel Feininger, Johannes Itten, and Oskar Schlemmer (pages 56, 68) each produced marvelously free, inventive posters seemingly unrelated to Bayer's austere compositions. (pages 65, 67). Yet all these artists shared a delight in the direct experimentation with letter forms, a freedom from traditional canons of composition, and a profoundly searching attitude towards design for machine production. This is nowhere better exemplified than in the experimental alphabets created by Bayer and Josef Albers (pages 55, 57).

In contrast to the posters of Bonnard and Lautrec, or to the work of the expressionists, the posters of the Bauhaus reveal little sense of the tactile pleasures of the print media. The luscious overlays of lithographic ink or the splintered gougings of the woodcut would be utterly out of place in this work, which used photoengraved illustrations and cleanly designed letterpress printing in place of the hand techniques of the previous generation.

Herbert Bayer (American, born
Austria, 1900).
Universal Type. 1925.

Piet Zwart. (Dutch, born 1885).
Three advertisements for N. V.
Nederlandsche Kabelfabriek. 1927–28?

Piet Zwart
Page from N. V. Nederlandsche
Kabelfabriek catalogue. 1928.
Gift of Philip Johnson.

H. N. Werkman (Hendrik Nicolaas
Werkman; Dutch, 1882–1945).
Composition. 1927–28?
Letterpress.

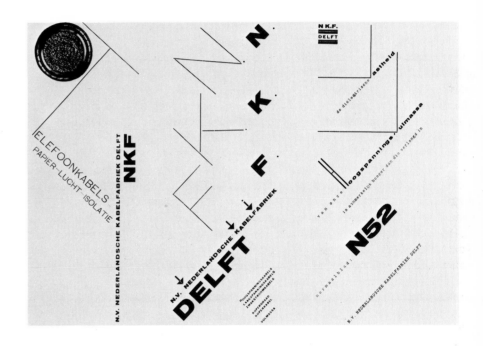

The same observations apply to the work that was being done in the
Netherlands during the 1920's. Dutch designers had arrived at some of their
conclusions independently, through the painting and design of such artists as
Theo van Doesburg and Piet Mondrian (who called their work *de Stijl),* although
they were not unaware of the growth of related design principles at the Bauhaus.
Certain differences – which seem minute and trivial, at this distance – tended to
keep the Dutch and German artists apart. But their work became better known
as the decade grew older, and such young artists as Piet Zwart and H.N.
Werkman followed their lead, and in some cases outshone them in poster and
typographic design. The artists of de Stijl were committed to the use of basic
colors, usually primaries, and uncompromisingly rectangular or square shapes.
The free exploration of forms and materials encouraged at the Bauhaus was not
tolerated by de Stijl. In the Netherlands it was left to Piet Zwart to develop his
sweeping typographical fantasies and photographic compositions (page 57),
and to Werkman to experiment with the free composition of miscellaneous sorts
of wood letters, rough printing blocks, and densely composed pages of type
of various sizes and forms.

A certain amount of experimentation along these lines had taken place in
France (with Apollinaire's poetry, for example), but until the artists of the 1920's
burst the bounds of traditional typography this had been the property of a tiny
group of the avant-garde. Now the style spread everywhere, and new artists
came to join in.

From Russia came the constructivists Malevich and Lissitzky, whose typographic
work came into full flower in the early twenties. Lissitzky joined the dadaist
Schwitters in 1924 in the publication of one of the fantastic publications of that
movement (page 56), and became a prime figure in the new art based on
letter forms that made no recognizable words.

It is not surprising that there should have been a connection between dada and
the new graphic design, for though dada artists rarely designed posters, their
symbolic language was very closely related to the new conception of the
poster. [26] Artists such as Raoul Hausmann, Marius de Zayas, Francis Picabia, and
Marcel Duchamp delighted in the use of familiar things in an allusive,
metaphorical way (page 59). Type is arranged in pictorial form, or pictures of
machine parts are recomposed to make new images. Picabia's *Machine tournez
vite* of 1916-1917[27] comes close to Lucian Bernhard in composition and color.
Other dada experiments with optical phenomena seem to anticipate Cassandre's
posters (as well as today's optical art), and – as we shall see presently – their
work found its expression in the photographic poster as well.

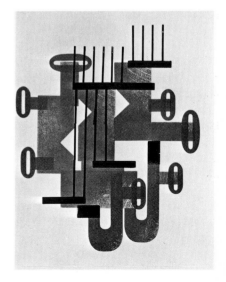

ZUM KRISENPARTEITAG DER S.P.D.

The use of photography as an illustrative medium in posters and magazines is taken for granted today. However, the union of the photograph and the typographic arts – in a freely creative sense, at least – only dates from the 1920's. Nor was it universally adopted then; few British or American poster designers of that decade seemed interested in utilizing photography, and none of the important patrons of the poster in those countries encouraged its use.

The best of the earlier pictorial posters were notable for their fantasy, wit, and color. These qualities were all antithetical to the standards of creative photographers at the turn of the century. Such photographers as Alfred Stieglitz, P.H. Emerson, or Frederick Evans, worked in comparatively sombre tones, cherished the small scale of the photograph, and were concerned with the assertion of specifically "photographic" qualities; moreover, the photomechanical reproductive processes essential to the production of economically printed posters destroyed the tonal gradations and surface qualities these photographers had labored so hard to achieve.

At the same time that the attitudes of poster artists and graphic designers were changing, around the time of the First World War, the technology of photoengraving improved. The heightened naturalism of such artists as Louis Raemaekers and Frank Brangwyn – and their ability to use black and white effectively in posters – suggested to photographers like Arnold Genthe that photographic illustration might be appropriate if used in this evocative, naturalistic sense. In Genthe's poster of 1917 (page 59), and others of its kind, the photograph stands by itself, like a framed picture unconnected with the textual elements of the composition; but at least this was a demonstration that the technology of printing could handle photographs sufficiently well to merit their serious consideration by the graphic designer.

Around 1920, perhaps motivated by the daring reassembly of the visible world undertaken by the cubists (particularly such later cubists as Robert Delaunay and Albert Gleizes), and entering into the spirit of formal innovation encouraged by the Bauhaus, de Stijl, and constructivism, a number of artists began to explore the possibilities of photographic techniques in the "new" graphic arts. As early as 1924, Piet Zwart combined photographs, flat tones, and sans-serif type into astonishing compositions in booklets for a broadcasting station and a cable manufacturer in the Netherlands. Zwart cut apart and reassembled photographic images in building his designs, but for the most part photographs were used unaltered until late in the decade. By then, the photograph was so generally accepted that Zwart was able to turn the tables, and evoke the motion picture in a witty combination of painted frames made to resemble a strip of film (page 69), while Max Burchartz was able to float violins across his photographic *Schubertfeier* poster (page 70).

It might have been expected that Germany, with its highly experimental photographers like László Moholy-Nagy and Albert Renger-Patzsch, would have led the field, but by far the most daring use of photography in posters in the late twenties and thirties was found in a few examples from the Soviet Union. Considering the lack of enthusiasm for earlier avant-garde posters in Russia, it may seem curious that such experimentation should occur ten years later. There is not sufficient evidence about Soviet art of the period to allow a complete explanation here, but it is possible that a reliance on photography seemed to make this work more accessible to the "ordinary man." Moreover, for a few years before 1935 there was a slight thaw in the centralized cultural control of art in the Soviet Union, and this may have encouraged a new spirit of graphic experimentation.

Whatever the causes, the results were quite remarkable. Klutsis, for example, simply used straight photographic images as the illustrative matter of his posters (pages 72–73), achieving power and vitality in his strongly diagonal compositions. Lissitzky, in contrast, started with straightforward photographs but altered them – especially in scale – to make a rather monumental and unsettling image (page 73). Still another use of the photograph is found in the posters of Boris Prusakov (page 72), who cut photographic images apart and reassembled them into witty and provocative montages.

Photomontage, the technique of assembling portions of various photographs into a new image, is capable of a particularly compelling and devastating impact. The persuasive power of even a small portion of a photograph is considerable, and if such highly charged bits are knowingly combined, an eloquent message emerges.

As might be expected, the origins of such a powerful technique are obscured in conflicting claims of priority and invention. George Grosz and John Heartfield, according to Grosz,[28] invented photomontage in 1916. Heartfield's partisans accord him a slight priority. Alexander Rodchenko's efforts in the Soviet Union at about the same time were hailed as pioneer efforts. The fact is that amateur efforts at photomontage (with all the qualities of wit and surprise we associate with the most sophisticated dada work) have been traced back as far as the 1860's.[29] Henry P. Robinson also assembled separate images in his elaborately printed photographic history pictures, and photomontage was described and illustrated in 1896 in the popular book *Photographic Amusements*.[30]

An invention ahead of its time usually is not fully used, and if the dada and surrealist artists cannot claim to have invented the technique of photomontage, at least they used it with unprecedented power and clarity. John Heartfield, like George Grosz and Otto Dix, took the tools of dada into the realm of social criticism (page 58); in Peter Selz's words, he "consciously placed photography

Raoul Hausmann (Austrian, born 1886).
Tatlin at Home. 1920.
Pasted photo-engravings, gouache, and pen and ink, 16⅛ x 11 inches.
Moderna Musset, Stockholm.

John Heartfield (Helmut Herzfeld; German, 1891–1968).
To The Party Convention of the S.P.D. 1931.

Arnold Genthe (American, born Germany, 1869–1942).
A Masque of the Red Cross. 1918.
Lithograph, 31¼ x 19 inches.
Acquired by exchange.

England between the Wars

in the service of political agitation.''[31] Always in the service of humanitarian radicalism from 1918, he brought new vitality and violence into his work after 1929, as the power of his primary target, Hitler, increased.
No more eloquent way could be found to express the emotional range of this technique than to compare the work of Heartfield with the beguiling photomontage posters of Herbert Matter (pages 74 – 75), which are almost exactly contemporary. Matter evokes the clear sky and white snow of Switzerland in a manner that emphatically asserts the modernity and sophistication of the country. Matter was able to reduce forceful and complex subjects to elemental visual terms, just as artists such as McKnight Kauffer (see page 77) did in their painted designs.
Typographically, these photographic posters display their modernity in the almost universal use of sans-serif letters – whether in Cyrillic or roman – and in the heavy rules and arcs used as decorative elements. But once this simple observation is made, it is astonishing to notice the variety of letter forms available to the designer within these limits, and the amount of expressive character extracted from these basically simple alphabets. Jan Tschichold uses an interestingly squared-off letter in his Buster Keaton poster (page 69); Zwart reduces his letter to a dangerously thin straight line in *ITF Film* (page 69); Matter expands and condenses his type. The sans-serif letter was shaded, incised, put into perspective, and turned on its side. It emerged as one of the most durable typographic revivals of the twenties and thirties.

Since the poster is among other things an advertising medium, it is not surprising that from time to time a particularly enlightened business executive should play an important role in the history of display typography and graphic design. Perhaps it is only surprising that this does not happen more frequently! The Tropon management gave van de Velde an unprecedented opportunity to create a series of industrial designs. The Allgemeine Elektrizitäts Gesellschaft commissioned Peter Behrens to design everything for the company from its building to its letterhead.
Similarly, Frank Pick of the London Underground Railways created a poster campaign notable for its generally high level of design, its use of advanced artists (even if they were unfashionable), and for its endurance.
Soon after his arrival in London in 1906, to join the administration of one of the newly created underground systems, Pick convinced his colleagues that stations – like shops – should have "front windows" advertising the delights to be found along the route.[32] The earliest posters are not extraordinary, keeping as they do to the predominant illustrative style of the times, but the campaign was unique. Moreover, Pick was concerned with the dual aspects of practicality and corporate uniformity of design, and sought assistance from some of England's best designers in planning the trains, station structures, and appurtenances required by the expanding railroad. The men he consulted improved his taste, and engendered an adventurous series of commissions.
For example, Edward Johnston was asked in 1915 to design a typeface for general use on vehicles and structures. This was a most unlikely choice, since Johnston's work had been almost exclusively in calligraphy. He was far from interested in commercial typography, and had serious reservations about his ability to undertake the design of a type. From all the evidence of his work to date, he could have been expected to produce a design in the spirit of the fifteenth or sixteenth centuries (or, for that matter, to go back to the time of Charlemagne). But Pick believed that he had found in Johnston a superb theorist of letter design, and he was not disappointed. The resulting London Underground Type of 1916 (page 60) was the first sans-serif type to be cut in the twentieth century from truly new designs; it is the ancestor of Gill Sans and Futura, and it is so well conceived that it is still in use today without any appreciable signs of age. Sans-serif type was meanwhile introduced into German typography independently of Johnston's work; it is fascinating to see how closely Johnston's geometrical experiments for the construction of letters based on classical roman proportions resemble the ruler-and-compass efforts of Herbert Bayer at the Bauhaus (page 57).[33]
With his newly developed sense of style and modernity, Pick now turned to a new group of artists for his posters. Perhaps the most prominent of these was

ABCDEFGHIJKLMN OPQRSTUVWXYZ abcdefghijklmnopq rstuvwxyz 123456 7890 (&£.,:;'!?-*"")

E. McKnight Kauffer, a young American illustrator who had come to work in London fired by the example of the new European art he had seen at the Armory Show during its Chicago showing in 1913. Pick discovered him in 1915 and gave him one of his first poster commissions.

Kauffer's earliest important poster design, strangely enough, was created without a specific client in mind. It is a remarkable flight of birds (page 78), built of an irregular series of triangles and parallelograms, using only three colors. This extraordinary composition bears some relationship to the cubism of Delaunay that Kauffer had seen in the 1913 Armory Show, and to the woodcuts of the Englishmen Robert Gibbings and Edward Wadsworth, but it transcended its models and took on a brilliant life of its own. Designed in 1915–1916, it was only published three years later (with lettering disowned by Kauffer[34]) as an advertisement for the Labour Party's *Daily Herald*. It was an immediate sensation. By 1920 Kauffer was working for a variety of clients along with the Underground, including Shell-Mex/BP (page 79) and Vigil Silk, but he never forgot his debt to Pick and gave him some of his finest designs (page 77). Kauffer was never committed to a single style. At one moment he used the rectilinear, disciplined shapes of the Bauhaus; another poster might be more in the spirit of Hohlwein. But Kauffer was never merely derivative, since he transformed these styles into a new and powerful mode of expression. Perhaps his greatest skill was his simplification of machine forms, suggesting in bold and legible compositions the power and movement of electrical generators or reciprocating engines. In his handling of lettering he was equally versatile.

Kauffer was by no means the only important artist to work for the London Underground. Pick commissioned posters by Frank Brangwyn, John Farleigh, Edward Bawden, Graham Sutherland, and scores of others. Man Ray – as improbably chosen as Edward Johnston, if for different reasons – produced a strikingly bold poster (page 85) using the Underground symbol (which Johnston had redesigned) as a planet in the firmament. László Moholy-Nagy, recently at the Bauhaus and newly in exile from Hitler's Germany, also was commissioned to do a series of posters for the Underground.

The program went on, after Frank Pick's death, with distinguished work by such artists as Zero (Hans Schleger), R. F. K. Henrion, Lewit-Him, and others in the great tradition of the early days. It continues today, less radical and pioneering perhaps, but still a source of pleasure to the London commuter.

For all the internationalism of art in the early twentieth century, certain contributions to the modern style simply did not travel well enough to flourish in another atmosphere. The formalism of the Russians and Germans, for example, made very little impact in France. In its place, several French designers evolved a bold, witty style that resembled nothing else being done, but made a deep impression on later artists – Swiss and American as well as French. Cassandre, in his *Nord Express* poster (page 80), obviously belongs to the generation of Kauffer and Klutsis, but some of the assertiveness of their imagery is softened and modified. Cassandre was an artist of immense gifts and individuality that could not be suppressed by mannerism. By the 1930's he emerged as one of the most influential designers at work, and may be said to have shifted the center of graphic design west of the Rhine.

Born Adolphe Mouron of French parents in Russia, Cassandre studied in Paris and in 1922 (at the age of 21) turned to poster designing. He soon was well known in France, and was able to influence the content of the advertising campaigns in which his work was used.

"A poster is above all a *word,*" wrote Cassandre around 1943, "…but there must be created around that word a series of associations of simple ideas."[35] In his design for the cover of a Museum of Modern Art exhibition of his work in 1936 (page 61), Cassandre demonstrated this principle with great economy; the poster is an arrow, piercing the eye of the beholder. One is reminded of Walter Crane's diatribe against poster designing; but Cassandre accepted the limitations of the medium and the commercial demands of the advertiser that Crane found degrading, and added an elegance of imagery and economy of visual statement previously absent from graphic design.

In more complex works, such as the poster for Triplex (page 80), this is seen at a more sophisticated stage of development. The reduction of text is accompanied by the expression of the product or service in purely visual terms. The driver behind the safety glass tells the viewer immediately what is being advertised. Perhaps Cassandre's most durable poster is his *Dubo Dubon Dubonnet* (page 81), first conceived in 1932 as a single figure and later expanded to its classic three-stage picture story. One is so enchanted by the immediately grasped idea – "Dubious – It's good – The name of the wine" – that the subtleties of the conception may go unnoticed. But it is precisely the rolling eye (simply rendered as a disc within a circle), the warm color suffusing the drinker by stages as the word fills out with color, and the immobility of the body in contrast to the shifts in position of hand, head, and eye that bear the imprint of Cassandre's genius as a poster designer.

Some of these same qualities are found in his type designs (for the Peignot foundry), his stage sets, and his magazine illustrations, which brought him work

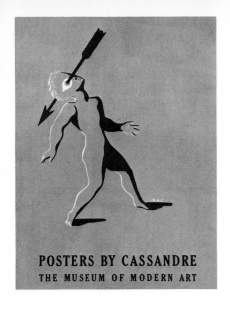

POSTERS BY CASSANDRE
THE MUSEUM OF MODERN ART

Edward Johnston (English,
1872–1944).
Sans serif alphabet designed for
London Transport. 1916.

A. M. Cassandre (Adolphe Mouron;
French, born Russia, 1901–1968).
Cover for exhibition catalogue.1936.

Jean Carlu (French, born 1900).
Give 'em Both Barrels. 1941.
Offset lithograph, 30 x 40 inches.
Gift of the Office of Emergency
Management.

in the United States as well as France; but his most important work remained
his posters which were used the world over.

I do not mean to suggest that Cassandre limited himself to a single approach to
poster design (*see* page 82 for a quite different style), or that he did not reflect
the avant-garde art of his time when it suited the job at hand. The brilliant
design of his *Nicolas* poster (page 83), which occupies a place midway between
McKnight Kauffer's flight of birds and the op art of the 1960's, is unforgettably
arresting. As with many of Cassandre's other posters, *Nicolas* found its
immediate reflection in such works as Jacques Nathan-Garamond's *Mazda
Platina* (page 85). It is instructive to compare these geometric designs with
the work of the Bauhaus and de Stijl, to see how the French designers relied on
allusiveness and elaboration that their German and Dutch colleagues scorned.
To devote this much space to Cassandre's work underscores his unusually
effective position, but it should not detract from the later impact of his work
on such younger French artists as Jean Carlu and Raymond Savignac, who have
made their own contributions to the art of the poster within the framework of
a similarly condensed, witty style.

"The memory retains everything that astonishes it," wrote Carlu,[36] and in his
posters can be found a multitude of images conceived with the intention of
arresting the eye of the viewer – and thus impressing his mind. Like Cassandre,
Carlu used a technique of painting that reproduced in an "unpainterly" fashion
(to borrow a term from Wölfflin). In contrast to the expressive roughness of the
German expressionists, these posters seem to bear no mark of the designer's
hand; colors and shapes either end precisely or flow off in utterly smooth
gradations. Hand lettering is indistinguishable from type in its regularity and
perfection. What is arresting in the imagery has sprung from the artist's
imagination, to be sure, but does not acquire power from the artist's passionate
rendition as do the posters of Kollwitz or Kokoschka.

Carlu preferred to be surprising. The wrench in his *Production* poster grasps the
the 'O' of the caption (page 93); a visual analogy is found between a machine
gun and a rivet-gun (page 61). Savignac (page 94), by contrast, is invariably
witty. A drink gushes from the bottle with a force that knocks the hat from the
drinker's head; the two figures in the *Astral* poster paint one another with the
advertiser's enamel in a conception worthy of Saul Steinberg or M. C. Escher.
One sees in these works the translation of surrealist imagery into advertising
design. Tanguy and Dali, for example, also minimized the appearance of
brushwork, and created surprising juxtapositions of objects seen with total
clarity, and exaggerated or abandoned the traditional canons of spatial
representation – all characteristics of these French posters, and new ingredients
in the art.

GIVE 'EM

BOTH BARRELS

During the 1930's the style of Cassandre and his colleagues began to make its mark among American graphic designers, accompanying a remarkable resurgence of vitality in graphic design in this country. After 1918, as the ferment of styles took place in Europe, avant-garde American designers found their own country far less receptive to new work than it had been in the days of Will Bradley, Penfield, and Sloan. McKnight Kauffer was unable to find any American client as willing to commission his work as London Transport or Shell-Mex was, when he returned briefly to the United States in 1921, and the young artists who came from America to work at the Bauhaus found it more rewarding (at least until the advent of Hitler) to continue working in Germany. In the thirties, however, several factors combined to change the American artistic climate. Through their work for slick magazines and a few American (and more international) advertisers, Cassandre and Carlu became known to the American public. New magazines such as *Fortune* took graphic design very seriously and commissioned the most inventive work they could find. Above all, there was the Depression.

Several projects sponsored by the Federal Government were devoted to the design and production of posters. In one of these the process of silk-screen printing, serigraphy, was perfected by the Velonis brothers and their co-workers in New York, and publicized through a handbook[37] and through the wide distribution of work done in the new technique. This project was to bear even richer fruit after the war.

Some of the new programs instituted to build the economy required posters, and helped to create a demand for better design for this purpose. Just as war and revolution fifteen years before had spurred designers in Europe, now depression and social reform had the same effect in the United States. A 1937 poster by Lester Beall for the Rural Electrification administration (page 87) is a good illustration of how the simplified forms, direct message, and smooth surfaces of Cassandre found an echo here. With the approach of World War II such typographers and illustrators as John Atherton, Glenn Grohe, Joseph Binder, and Henry Koerner enlisted these formal resources in the service of mobilization and propaganda (pages 87–89).

Naturally this was not the only outside force in the new American poster work. A number of the former Bauhaus staff had been forced to emigrate when political pressures closed the school in Dessau, and had come to the United States. Lester Beall's *Cross Out Slums* (page 86) is related to Herbert Bayer's *Wohnung* poster (page 66) not only in its simple motif of rejection but also in its use of photography and sans-serif letters, although the hand holding the chalk is more nearly a descendent of Carlu's or Savignac's simplified draughtsmanship. The early work of such talented designers as Beall is filled

with this mixture of new ideas, but soon the ideas were assimilated – along with the exiled European designers – and an entirely new spirit was infused into American graphic design.

Herbert Matter arrived in the States in 1936, and with Beall, Leo Lionni (page 90), and Milton Ackoff, carried photographic poster illustration to new heights of inventiveness. These and other American designers were able to bring the clean asymmetry of Bauhaus design into everyday life in this country long before Gropius and Mies Van der Rohe were given an opportunity to do so in architecture.

Entirely apart from these artists, who came to the poster from industrial design and typography, is the remarkable work of Ben Shahn. Shahn had been trained as a commercial lithographer and lettering artist, but had long since abandoned this for painting and drawing when depression and then war gripped the country. In 1936 he turned a tempera painting derived from his experiences as a photographer for the Resettlement Administration into a powerful poster (page 86) – this was the first of a series of posters aimed at political and social targets, a series that Shahn is still producing. In the 1940's came a series of posters for the CIO Political Action Committee and for the war effort (pages 91, 92), in which Shahn used his skill as an illustrator to create memorable, bold designs that are notable for their incorporation of the painter's direct brushwork into images as arresting as the polished forms of Kauffer and Cassandre, but with more passion and personal engagement.

With his interest in lettering, it is not surprising that Shahn should have investigated alternatives to the sans-serif letter, which had become almost obligatory. In *This is Nazi Brutality* (page 91) the strips of the teletype printer contribute a sense of authenticity and immediacy, and in his postwar designs (page 100) Shahn has utilized a highly individualistic thick-and-thin letter in which the roman letter is given bold stress reminiscent of the Hebrew alphabet for which Shahn has always had a deep affection. Shahn describes this as an "amateur or folk alphabet," which he had begun to study in the 1930's as he made photographs around the country for the Federal Government.[38]

After the war, as the economy began to recover and the new generation of graphic artists turned to activities over which they might have more control, the design profession became organized in the United States as it never had before. Advertising agencies, free-lance designers, small groups of artists all became involved in poster and typographic work, and the demand for their services has grown continuously up to the present. A comparable development took place in Europe, particularly in Switzerland and Great Britain, and – as we shall see in the following sections – other nations have produced designers and poster artists where these activities were previously of little significance.

Joost Schmidt (German, 1893–1942).

Staatliches Bauhaus Ausstellung. 1923.
Lithograph, 26¼ x 18⅝ inches.
Gift of Walter Gropius.

Walter Dexel (German, born 1890).

Fotografie Der Gegenwart. 1929.
Linocut, 33¼ x 23¼ inches.
Gift of the designer.

Walter Dexel.

Verwende Stets Nur Gas (Use Only Gas). 1924.
Letterpress, 19 x 25 inches.
Purchase fund.

Herbert Bayer (American, born Austria, 1900).

Architektur Lichtbilder Vortrag Professor Hans Poelzig. 1926.
Letterpress, 18¾ x 25½ inches.
Gift of Philip Johnson.

Herbert Bayer.

Wie Wohnen? Die Wohnung Werkbund Ausstellung (How Would You Like To Live? An Exhibition of Interiors). 1927.
Offset lithograph, 35¼ x 32⅜ inches.
Gift of Mr. and Mrs. Alfred H. Barr, Jr.

Herbert Bayer.

Ausstellung Europäisches Kunstgewerbe 1927 Leipzig (European Arts and Crafts Exhibition Leipzig 1927).
Offset lithograph, 35¼ x 23¾ inches.
Gift of Mr. and Mrs. Alfred H. Barr, Jr.

Herbert Bayer.

Kandinsky zum 60. Geburtstag (Kandinsky on His 60th Birthday). 1926.
Offset lithograph, 19 x 25 inches.
Gift of Mr. and Mrs. Alfred H. Barr, Jr.

Oskar Schlemmer (German, 1888–1943).

Grosse Brücken Revue (Big Bridges Review). 1926.
Lithograph, 46½ x 38½ inches.
Purchase fund.

C.O.Muller (German, born 1893).

Im 7. Himmel Phoebus Palast (Seventh Heaven). 1927.
Linoleum cut, 46½ x 32¼ inches.
Gift of Mr. and Mrs. Alfred H. Barr, Jr.

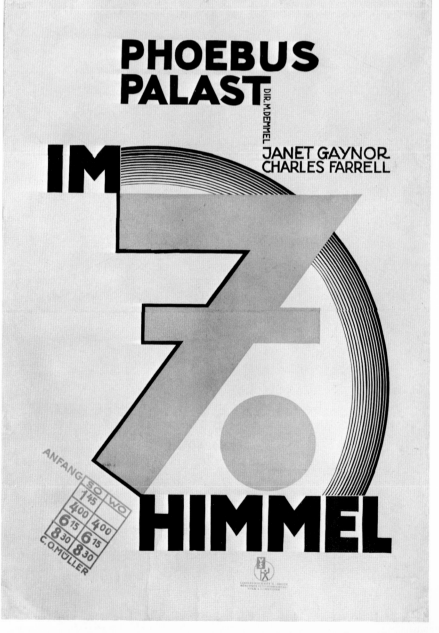

Jan Tschichold (German, born 1902).

Buster Keaton in: "Der General". 1927.
Offset lithograph, 47¾ x 32½ inches.
Gift of the designer.

Piet Zwart (Dutch, born 1885).

ITF Internationale Tentoonstelling op Filmgebied. 1928.
Lithograph, 42¼ x 30⅝ inches.
Anonymous gift.

Max Burchartz (German, born 1887).

Schubertfeier der Staedtischen Buehnen Essen (Schubert Festival). 1928.
Offset lithograph, 23¼ x 33 inches.
Gift of Philip Johnson.

Alexander Rodchenko (Russian, 1891–1956).

INGA (Theatre of the Revolution). 1920–1930.
Letterpress, 29¾ x 41¾ inches.
Gift of Jay Leyda.

Boris Prusakov (Russian).

I Hurry to See the Khaz Push. 1927.
Offset lithograph, 28 x 41½ inches.
Anonymous gift.

G. Klutsis (Russian).

Transport Achievement of the First Five-year Plan. 1929.
Gravure, 28⅞ x 19⅞ inches.
Purchase fund.

El Lissitzky (Eleazar Markovich; Russian, 1890–1941).

USSR Russische Ausstellung. 1929.
Gravure, 49 x 35¼ inches.
Gift of Philip Johnson.

G. Klutsis

Fulfilled Plan Great Work. 1930.
Gravure, 48⅝ x 33 inches.
Purchase fund.

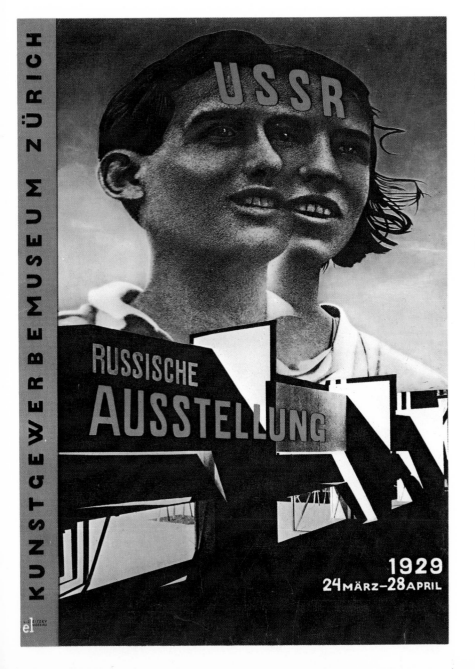

Herbert Matter (American, born Switzerland, 1907).

All Roads Lead to Switzerland. 1935.
Gravure, 39¾ x 25⅛ inches.
Gift of Bernard Davis.

Herbert Matter.

Winterferien–Doppelte Ferien Schweiz (Winter Vacations). 1936.
Gravure, 39¾ x 25⅛ inches.
Gift of G.E. Kidder Smith.

Herbert Matter.

Pontresina Engadin. 1935.
Gravure, 40 x 25⅛ inches.
Gift of the designer.

Herbert Matter.

Die Schweiz das grosse Erlebnis im Flugzeug (Switzerland. The Great Adventure by Plane). c. 1935.
Gravure, 40 x 25⅛ inches.
Gift of the designer.

Jan Tschichold.

Der Berufsphotograph Gewerbemuseum Basel (The Professional Photographer).
1938.
Offset lithograph, 24 x 35½ inches.
Gift of the designer.

E. McKnight Kauffer (American, 1890–1954).

Metropolis. 1926.
Tempera, 18½ x 29¾ inches.
Anonymous gift.

E. McKnight Kauffer.

Power the Nerve Centre of London's Underground. 1930.
Lithograph, 39½ x 25 inches.
Gift of the designer.

E. McKnight Kauffer.

Untitled. 1919.
Lithograph, 39¼ x 59⅝ inches.
Gift of the designer.

E. McKnight Kauffer.

E. McKnight Kauffer.

Magicians Prefer Shell. 1934.
Lithograph, 30 x 45 inches.
Gift of the designer.

A. M. Cassandre (Adolphe Mouron; French, born Russia, 1901–1968).

Chemin de Fer du Nord Nord Express. 1927.
Lithograph, 41 x 29¼ inches.
Gift of French National Railways.

A. M. Cassandre.

Triplex. 1930.
Lithograph, 47⅜ x 31⅜ inches.
Anonymous gift.

A. M. Cassandre.

Dubo Dubon Dubonnet. 1934.
Lithograph, 17½ x 45½ inches.
Gift of Bernard Davis.

A. M. Cassandre.

Chemin de Fer Du Nord Chantilly Lys. 1930.
Lithograph, 39¼ x 24⅝ inches.
Gift of G.E. Kidder Smith.

A. M. Cassandre.

Restaurez-vous au Wagon-Bar. 1932.
Lithograph, 39⅜ x 24⅜ inches.
Gift of Benjamin Weiss.

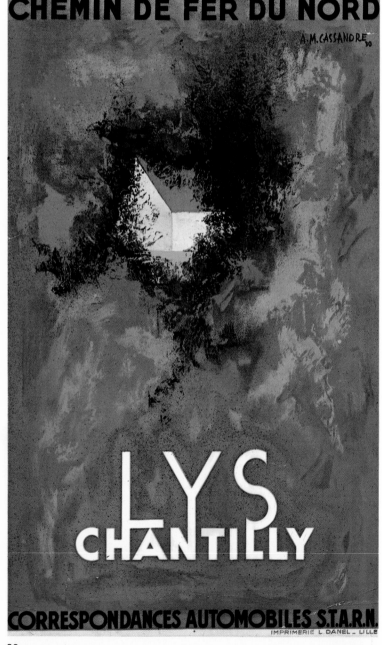

J. S. Anderson (British).

Motorists Prefer Shell. 1935.
Offset lithograph, 30 x 44¾ inches.
Anonymous gift.

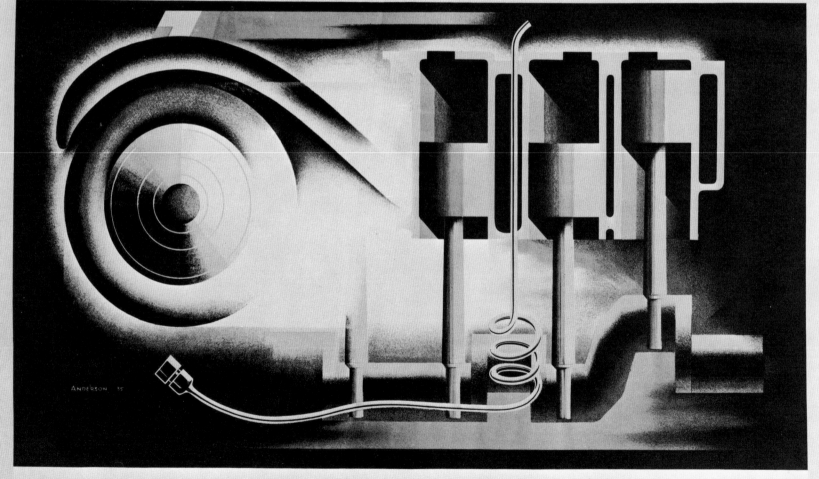

Jacques Nathan-Garamond (French, born 1910).

Elles les eclipse toutes Mazda Platina (They Eclipse All Others). c. 1938.
Offset lithograph, 45⅝ x 63 inches.
Gift of the designer.

Man Ray (American, born 1890).

Keeps London Going. 1932.
Offset lithograph, 39⅝ x 24¼ inches.
Gift of Bernard Davis.

Ben Shahn (American, born Lithuania, 1898).

Years of Dust. 1937.
Lithograph, 38 x 24¾ inches.
Gift of the designer.

Lester Beall (American, born 1903).

Cross out Slums. 1941.
Offset lithograph, 39½ x 29⅛ inches.
Gift of the designer.

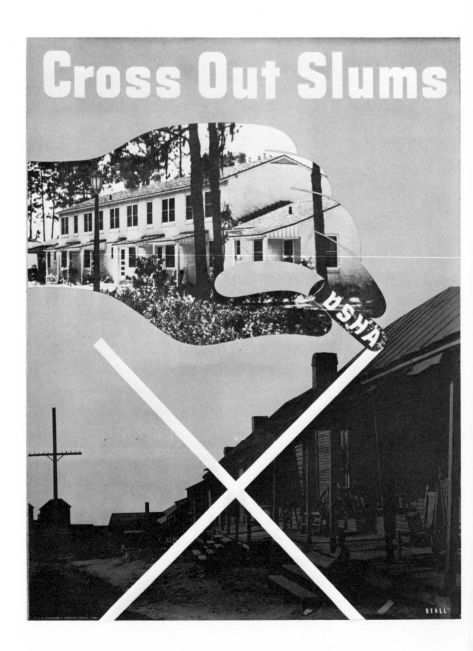

Lester Beall.

Running Water Rural Electrification Administration. 1937.
Silk screen, 40 x 30 inches.
Gift of the designer.

Joseph Binder (American, born Austria, 1898).

Air Corps U.S. Army. 1941.
Tempera, 40 x 30 inches.
Gift of the designer.

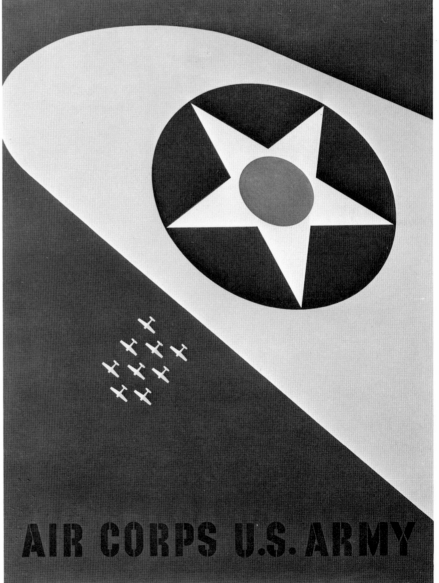

Henry Koerner (American, born Austria, 1915).

Someone Talked!
Offset lithograph, 32¾ x 23½ inches.
Gift of the designer.

Abram Games (English, born 1914).

Your Talk May Kill Your Comrades. 1943.
Offset lithograph, 29 x 18¾ inches.
Gift of the designer.

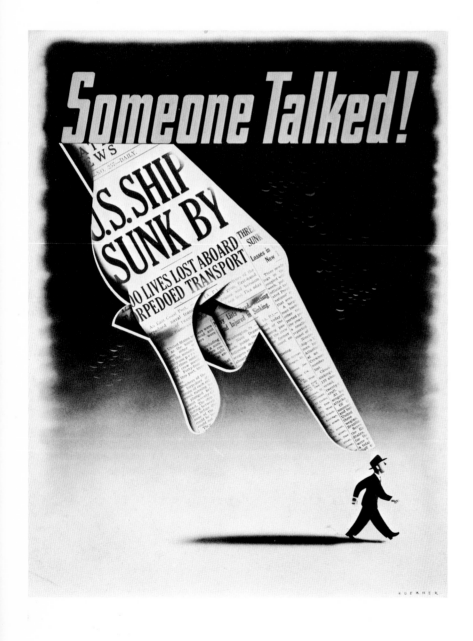

Glenn Grohe (American, born 1912).

He's Watching You. 1942.
Offset lithograph, 14⅛ x 10 inches.
Gift of the Office for Emergency Management.

Kukrinski:

Mikhail Kuprianov (Russian, born 1903),
Porfiry Krylov (Russian, born 1902), and
Nikolai Sokolov (Russian, born 1903).

Hitler Is Breaking Through the Non-agression Pact! 1941.
Lithograph, 34⅜ x 24½ inches.
Anonymous gift.

Charles Coiner (American, born 1898).

Give It Your Best! 1942.
Offset lithograph, 20 x 28½ inches.
Gift of the Office for Emergency Management.

Leo Lionni (American, born The Netherlands, 1910).

Keep 'Em Rolling! 1941.
Offset lithograph, 40 x 28⅛ inches.
Gift of the Office for Emergency Management.

Ben Shahn.

This Is Nazi Brutality. 1943.
Offset lithograph, 40⅛ x 28¼ inches.
Gift of the Office of War Information.

Ben Shahn.

Break Reaction's Grip Register Vote. 1944.
Offset lithograph, 44 x 29 inches.
Gift of S.S. Spivack.

Ben Shahn.

For Full Employment after the War Register Vote. 1944.
Offset lithograph, 30 x 37⅞ inches.
Gift of the CIO Political Action Committee.

Jean Carlu (French, born 1900).

America's Answer! Production. 1942.
Offset lithograph, 30 x 40 inches.
Gift of the Office for Emergency Management.

In this selective chronicle of poster history, it can be seen that the frenzied production and collecting activity of the 1890's gave way to more scattered activity (but perhaps the energies of the designers were channeled into more searching and thoughtful directions) once the Art Nouveau style had played itself out as a creative force. By 1930 the graphic designer began to regain a position in the art world *per se,* instead of having his poster and typographic work treated merely as an offshoot of his other interests. But the disabling effects of economic depression and war delayed the full second flowering of graphic design until the 1950's. Now we are in a renewed poster craze, which, interestingly enough, follows a revival of Art Nouveau; but the posters now so avidly collected are by no means restricted to those in the styles of the 1890's. Since the Second World War the lessons of the previous half century have been incorporated into a highly sophisticated, incredibly productive, and technically advanced graphic-arts technology. International boundaries mean less than stylistic creativity, and there is a frenzied demand for new appearances, new imagery, and new effects.

As the profession of graphic designer became defined, there developed a sense of the history of printing. Those concerned with type design and book typography during the first half of the century, like the late Stanley Morison or Daniel Berkeley Updike, defined the permissible limits of typographic freedom rather narrowly; but they pointed the way to the discovery of historical materials of far greater variety than they were willing to use in their own work. Starting in the 1930's, in England and in the Netherlands, there began to be a revival of nineteenth-century type faces that were notable for their allusive and evocative qualities. John Betjeman, James Shand, Robert Harling, Herbert Spencer, and the editors of the *Architectural Review* in London,[39] as well as H.N. Werkman in the Netherlands, cheerfully used the odd-shaped display letters of their grandfathers to give emphasis and impact to designs that were otherwise quite contemporary in character.

At the same time, printing technology itself was undergoing a quiet revolution. Before the war, experiments were under way to make the flexible technique of offset lithography produce sheets as well printed as letterpress could do. Silk screen found wider commercial applications, and mechanical silk screen printing devices were invented. Photolithographic materials were improved and made more available.

The war drove much of this activity underground, although the technological demands of the military hastened many developments. Werkman and another Dutchman, W. H. C. Sandberg, literally went underground, with the invasion of the Netherlands; elsewhere, artists and designers worked more openly for their governments, but had to yield to the demands of propaganda and work within

W. H. C. Sandberg (Willem Sandberg;
Dutch, born 1897).
Cover for NU In the Middle of the
Twentieth Century. 1959.
Gift of the designer.

Herbert Kapitzki (German, born 1925).
LGA-Zentrum Form. 1965.
Silkscreen, 33 x 23¾ inches.
Library of Congress, Washington, D.C.

Eugene Feldman (American, born
1929).
Poster for exhibition. 1962.
Offset lithograph, 31¼ x 19¼ inches.
Gift of the designer.

the limitations of shortages of materials, which made experimentation difficult or impossible. Despite these strictures, work effective in message and graphic imagery was produced in England, the United States, and the U.S.S.R. (pages 88–89).

Sandberg, for example, had experimented with Clarendon types, in place of the ubiquitous sans-serif, and found that they looked particularly well on ribbed brown wrapping paper; after the war, in his posters and catalogues for the Stedelijk Museum of Amsterdam (of which he was director), he made these materials a personal trademark (page 96).

Meanwhile, such younger designers in the Netherlands as Wim Crouwel and Pieter Brattinga were discovering the delights of greatly enlarged letter forms, which showed the irregularities of cutting and impression in imprecise edges, as a means of modifying the purity of their designs and imposing a sense of vibrancy and handwork on their book covers and posters (page 110).

Perhaps the most fascinating postwar development has been the appearance of a number of extremely talented designers in countries like Poland, Czechoslovakia, and Japan, previously undistinguished for their poster art. In Poland, for example, artists such as Jan Lenica, Roman Cieslewicz, Jan Mlodozoniec, Jerzy Panek, and Henryk Tomaszewski have produced bright and amusing circus posters, and some of the most inventive posters for theater and the film to be seen anywhere (pages 101–102). These are not particularly remarkable for their technique of reproduction; the paper is uniformly ordinary, and the lithographic and letterpress printing are no better than can be found in a score of countries. But the quality of imagery, draughtsmanship, simplicity, and free association of visual motifs is unique; Polish designers have explored the possibilities of freely designed letters and informal calligraphy more thoroughly than anyone else.

These artists seem more closely related to Savignac than to the Bauhaus. They have little interest in the niceties of geometric organization, or suiting their designs to machine production. Like their Czech contemporaries, their art comes out of a vital tradition of book illustration and painting, rather than from industrial design or architecture. It can also be related to the growth of the film art in recent years, and to lively teaching in the many art schools in Poland. Polish critics[40] attribute some of this vitality to their economic system, which, while it has failed to produce the strong recovery of the Western nations (and has engendered many scarcities of artists' materials and printing paper), has freed the artist from the necessity to *sell,* and permitted him to *comment* on the performance or occasion to which his design refers.

In Japan, by contrast, there appear to be greater affinities with the pure letter forms, disciplined geometrical design elements, and smooth surfaces that are associated with the German and Dutch designers of the twenties, although these characteristics are entirely transformed and brought up to date. Immediately after the war the struggles of Japanese designers to absorb a sense of roman letter design into their graphic art threatened to doom their efforts. With a burst of intelligent effort, however, the traditional virtues of simplicity, fitness to purpose, and harmony were reasserted, and grafted onto the new international abstract movement. Japanese graphic art was reborn. A remarkable poster by Ryuichi Yamashiro (page 101) is composed of a Japanese pictograph character that, alone, means "tree." A pair of these characters means "woods," and a trio means "forest." He has combined them in a composition that quite literally says "woods and forests," but at the same time suggests a tree-covered landscape. Other Japanese artists have used inventive combinations of metallic colors, dark papers, or photography – often printed in a velvety silk-screen process, with perfectly controlled colors and opacities of ink.

Another country in which the graphic arts have flourished is Switzerland. Grasset and Steinlen were of Swiss origin, but their contributions to the poster of the turn of the century were made in France. It is true that Swiss artists produced posters of high quality between 1900 and 1940, but these are generally in the character of work being done in Germany and France. Only in the 1940's did the influence of such teaching centers as the Kunstgewerbeschule in Zurich become truly significant, and begin to produce designers with a truly original approach. Another important factor was the determined effort of the Swiss Ministry of the Interior to improve poster art through a national competition (starting in 1942)[41] and through the standardization of poster display facilities throughout the Swiss Confederation so that these designs could be widely shown. Not only private advertisers and transportation facilities, but also local and canton governments in Switzerland (particularly Basel) have been enthusiastic patrons of the graphic arts, commissioning posters, booklets, stamps, brochures, signs, and letterheads in an unequalled utilization of design resources.

In a sense, the Swiss have built on the work of the Bauhaus. Jan Tschichold had designed brilliant "asymmetric" posters starting in the late 1920's (page 69); when his book *Asymmetric Typography* appeared in 1935 he demonstrated himself an eloquent apologist for the work of Lissitzky, Albers, and Van Doesburg, and a theorist of abstract art, photomontage, and decoration as well as typography. Some of Tschichold's designs from this period would be perfectly in keeping with Swiss work today, though in the intervening years he has amended many of his ideas and turned back to more classical typographical styles both in his book and display work.

Three parallel strands run through postwar Swiss poster designing. Imaginative and amusing posters using painted illustrations are produced by such artists as

Celestino Piatti, Donald Brun, and Herbert Leupin (page 104). Moody and powerful surrealist designs by Hans Erni, Armin Hoffmann, and others have been used for political and social campaigns with tremendous effectiveness (pages 106, 107). And typographic designers such as Josef Müller-Brockmann, Carlo Vivarelli, and Max Bill have given a particularly Swiss character to the use of newly designed sans-serif letters combined in orderly, carefully rendered designs, printed in the impeccable fashion for which Swiss presses have became famous (pages 108, 107, 105). Even when a more strident effect is attempted, as in Müller-Brockmann and Heiniger's safety poster (page 108), the design seems frozen in action in contrast to the rushing force achieved by a designer such as Klutsis (page 72). And among younger designers, Karl Gerstner combines the surrealistic and formalistic (page 106), mixing economy and logic of typography with photographic images that are oversize in scale and hypnotic in effect.

From postwar Germany comes a good deal of work that springs from the same origins (pages 111–113), but artists there were also among the earliest and most effective explorers in the field of optical effects in graphic design. Several years before the short-lived op art came on the scene, Almir Mavignier and Herbert Kapitzki in Germany were creating similar over-all geometrical patterns, and using colored and metallic areas in "hard-edge" compositions (pages 96, 118). Kapitzki had studied with Willi Baumeister, and although he had emerged from the painter's studio, he turned professionally to graphic design. Mavignier, on the other hand, arrived in Germany from Brazil determined to paint, but has since turned to graphic design with equal intensity – bringing to it some of the most effective optical experimentation to be found on the Continent. One is not surprised to learn that he studied with Max Bill and Josef Albers.

In Italy, immediately after the war, there occurred another example of enlightened industrial patronage of the graphic arts in the tradition of Tropon or the London Underground. In this case, the visionary Adriano Olivetti merged his graphic-arts campaign into a total social and commercial restructuring of his company; the design of products, of homes for the workers in his factories, and of the structure of the company itself was totally altered in the postwar era.[42] His art director, Giovanni Pintori, created a witty and inventive program of graphic design that at once conveyed both the image of Olivetti as a company and also the specific products it sold. Later, as Olivetti expanded its activities into the United States, the company engaged Leo Lionni to project its new spirit here.

In the United States since the forties, Lionni had been working with *Fortune* in New York and was one of those responsible for developing that magazine's clear graphic style. With a specially designed logotype, and with simplified figures created of flat shapes, he designed for Olivetti a series of posters and brochures (page 103) that proclaim a corporate identity and retain a unity of design while displaying diversity in message and conception. Today Olivetti's image continues to be projected through the work of Giovanni Pintori, Giorgio Soavi, and others (page 100).

In the United States, beginning in the late 1950's, the photolithographer Eugene Feldman has explored the surprising visual imagery resulting from the drastic enlargement of high-contrast photographic images combined with subtly controlled overprinting in color (page 97). Sometimes he loses the identity of his original image entirely, but he also achieves new combinations of shapes and colors from the successive printing of plates made at varying exposures, which re-create the sense of the image without reproducing it.

If Feldman tries to make us aware of the previously unseen qualities of the contemporary photographic image, another group of present-day Americans prefers to evoke nostalgia for a bygone era. Milton Glaser and his colleagues at the Push-Pin Studios in New York have long been exploring the potentialities of drawings rendered in brilliant colors, which gain strength and avoid clashing disaster through the use of bold outlines. The costumes, moustaches, and pointing fingers beloved of the Glaser group in one of its recent periods take us back to the horse-and-buggy days, but with such a sense of dash and vigor that their work has become exceptionally popular for book jackets, paperback covers, and small advertisements. In a more contemporary vein, Glaser's posters for Bob Dylan, WOR, and Mahalia Jackson (page 121) demonstrate this graphic personality. More recently, Peter Gee has turned to metallic inks and papers to achieve glittering effects (page 117). Many present-day designers in the United States favor droll and idiosyncratic lettering, inspired by everything from Shahn's folk alphabets to the display types of the 1920's or the more extreme letter designs of Art Nouveau.

In a sense, this smacks of "found art" – springing from the same impulse that motivated Picasso and Schwitters to use letters three or four decades ago – but it is also involved with a growing feeling that legibility is an unimportant concern in the design of a graphic "object." For we are no longer thinking of the poster as solely a medium for the transmission of ideas, or information, or a sales message. Posters in this sense have become printed paintings, or mass-produced prints: the direct expression of an artist's feelings or responses to the visual devices at his command.

Perhaps this is most emphatically seen in the recent appearance of "psychedelic" posters (pages 124–126), fusing elements of the Art Nouveau revival with newly available luminous and transparent inks to create images of shattering vibrancy and activity. In place of the languid rhythms of Art Nouveau, the psychedelic designer invests his design with restless energy. In place of

Henri Matisse (French, 1869–1954).
Nice Travail Joie H. Matisse. 1947.
Lithograph, 39½ x 25⅜ inches.
Gift of G. E. Kidder Smith.

Art Nouveau's intangible form and indefinable color, the new poster assaults the senses with a profusion of explicit stimuli. The message is loud, usually irreverent, and often confusing; posters for musical events and political groups carry equally illegible captions, almost as if the artist defies his viewer to try to find the words in the midst of his design. And in the wake of the genuine products of the LSD culture of San Francisco, the psychedelic style has swept the "hippy" world into the advertising offices of the New York and London.
It is not surprising that a few young Japanese artists, of whom Tadanori Yokoo is perhaps the most inventive (pages 126–127), should have found the psychedelic style sympathetic, since it has picked up the aniline-dye brilliance and frenzied activity of popular Japanese art of the past fifty years. Yokoo has increased the frenzy and glare to an almost unbearable point, so that one nearly misses the sly references to classical Japanese motifs and erotic images. Again, his "posters" often do not advertise anything, but become a new form of graphic communication.
Yet another fascinating component of the present activity in poster design is the artist's poster – advertising an exhibition, or using the unmodified work of a painter to announce a cultural event. Although Bonnard, Grasset, and others in the 1890's and early 1900's designed posters for their own exhibitions, the artist's poster is primarily a phenomenon of the postwar period. Shortly after 1945, perhaps in an attempt to call attention to the resumption of a normal cultural life, a few galleries in Paris called on their artists to provide posters.
In collaboration with the lithographic studios of Mourlot and Lacourière, posters advertising exhibitions by Miró, Picasso, Matisse, and Braque were issued, and these burst upon the art world with surprising results (pages 128–130). They were collected as avidly as the more serious works by the artists, and even large editions were soon exhausted. The French National Tourist Office, quick to react to this striking phenomenon, adapted a luminous Matisse painting into a superb poster (page 98), and added it to an elegant series of photographic tourist advertisements.
Soon there was a considerable market for artists' posters, with both commercial galleries and museums commissioning distinguished work. The earlier posters generally used a picture in isolation from the text, sometimes even enclosing the illustration in a frame. Miró and Braque, perhaps recalling the lessons of their predecessors in Paris, showed that these posters could be even more effective if the artist incorporated his own lettering into the design. In the past decade, artists as diverse as Jean Dubuffet and Frank Stella have contributed memorable designs to the growing number of artist's posters (pages 135, 138), and half a dozen shops across the nation are hard put to satisfy the demand for this kind of art.

It is a paradox that today, when there is so much exploration and activity in the field of poster design, there should be so few places for the public display of posters. Apart from the subway station, airport, or theater billboard, places to mount posters have become practically nonexistent; one need only walk down Fifth Avenue, or Michigan Avenue, to sense this, and perhaps this is why the graphic designer has been exploring new functions for the poster. Having lost its role as an arrestor of the public eye, the poster is now in the process of becoming a print medium; Walter Crane would find himself today largely freed from the necessity to compromise with his clients.
In its hundred years of existence, the poster has surely justified itself. Through Art Nouveau, in all its manifestations across Europe, and particularly through the thought and work of such leaders as van de Velde, graphic design came to be automatically included in the sphere of total design that was to be the basis of a productive art and society. Behrens, Olbrich, and their students, along with their contemporaries in the Netherlands, carried the total-design theories, if not the forms, of Art Nouveau into a powerfully influential movement.
Others kept the painter's hand in the poster, feeling that it was a powerful means of expression and communication. Kandinsky, Pechstein, and Kollwitz were less concerned with saying anything about how all art should be created than with making a moving public statement.
As the twentieth century grew older, this divergence of theory and form – between the painter/designer and the designer/graphic-artist – widened, until today there seem to be two arts of the poster. Between these poles are the young, exploring designer/artists, testing the potentialities of new ways of seeing, printing, and shaping the graphic arts. It may well be that their search for a new graphic art is an occurrence as important as the search for new form in which the Bauhaus and the constructivists were engaged; finding materials and idioms appropriate to the expression of new ideas, freeing the poster from the polarity of "painting" and "design," today's designers may be leading us into an entirely new world.
If this is true, then the poster as we have known it will cease to exist. It will have had a history of exactly one century, engaging the talents of some of the most important artists of ten exceedingly interesting decades. In its familiar form, as we see it in this book, the poster has evolved into a matchless medium for the communication of simply stated, basic ideas and powerful emotions. It has proved its power to arrest the eye, and to inform in a direct manner. And it has given the world a group of art objects of singular beauty, force, and wit.

Raymond Savignac (French, born 1907).

L'Eau qui fait pschitt. 1950.
Offset lithograph, 90¼ x 62¾ inches.
Gift of the designer.

Raymond Savignac.

Astral Peinture Email. 1949.
Offset lithograph, 58¾ x 39¼ inches.
Gift of the designer.

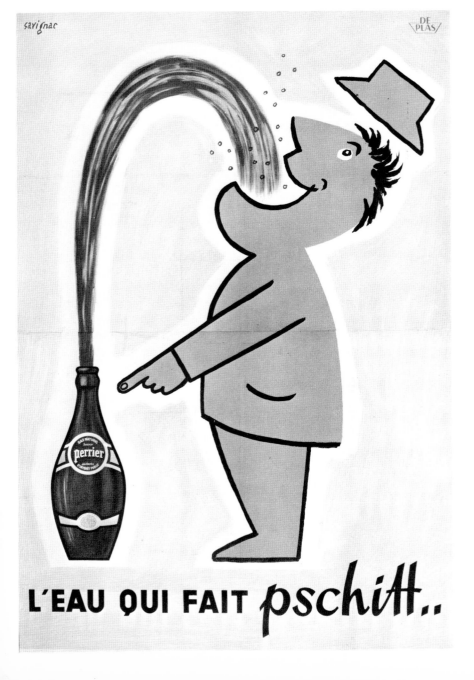

Ben Shahn.

Ballets U.S.A. 1959.
Silk screen and offset lithograph, 31⅜ x 21¼ inches.
Anonymous gift.

Giovanni Pintori (Italian, born 1912).

Olivetti Tetractys. 1957.
Offset lithograph, 27¾ x 19½ inches.
Gift of the Olivetti Company.

EXHIBIT-JEROME ROBBINS "BALLETS U.S.A."-U.S.I.S. GALLERY 41 GROSVENOR SQ. LONDON W.1. SEPT. 15-OCT. 23, 1959

Olivetti Tetractys. 1957.

Leo Lionni.

Olivetti Lettera 22. 1956.
Silk screen, 26⅜ x 18¾ inches.
Gift of the Olivetti Company.

Jan Mlodozoniec (Polish, born 1929).

Cyrk (Circus). 1966.
Offset lithograph, 37 x 26¼ inches.
Gift of the designer.

Roman Cieslewicz (Polish, born 1930).

Strawinski Persefona. 1961.
Offset lithograph and gravure, 38 x 26⅝ inches.
Gift of the designer.

Jan Lenica (Polish, born 1928).

Cena Strachu (The Wages of Fear). 1958.
Offset lithograph, 33¼ x 22¼ inches.
Gift of Mr. and Mrs. Jerzy Michalowski.

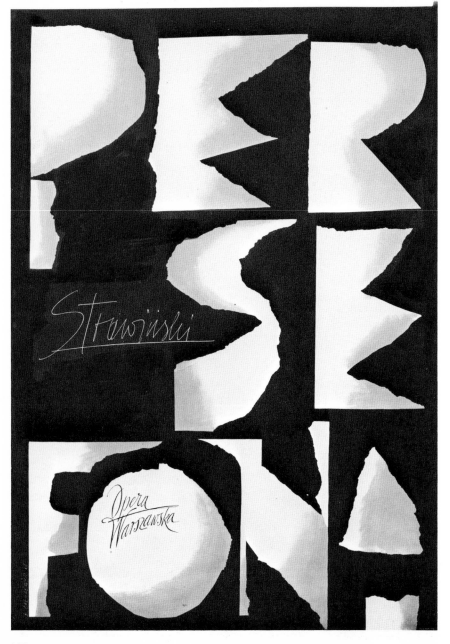

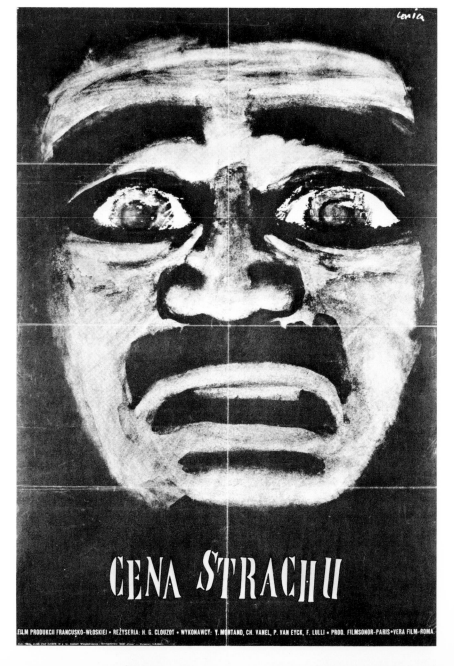

Ryuichi Yamashiro (Japanese, born 1920).

Forest. 1954.
Silk screen, 41 x 29½ inches.
Gift of the designer.

Paul Rand (American, born 1914).

Interfaith Day. 1954.
Offset lithograph, 45 x 29 inches.
Gift of the designer.

Herbert Leupin (Swiss, born 1916).

...trink lieber Eptinger! (instead drink Eptinger). 1948.
Offset lithograph, 50¼ x 35¼ inches.
Gift of Swiss Commercial Extension Office, Lausanne.

Donald Brun (Swiss, born 1909).

Internationale Musikfest Wochen Luzern (International Music Festival Week Lucerne). 1950.
Offset lithograph, 50¼ x 35⅜ inches.
Gift of Kunstgewerbemuseum, Zurich.

Jan Tschichold.

Konstruktivisten Kunsthalle Basel. 1937.
Offset lithograph, 51¾ x 35½ inches.
Purchase fund.

Max Bill (Swiss, born 1908).

Futurismo & Pittura Metafisica Kunsthaus Zurich. 1950.
Offset lithograph, 39¼ x 27½ inches.
Gift of the designer.

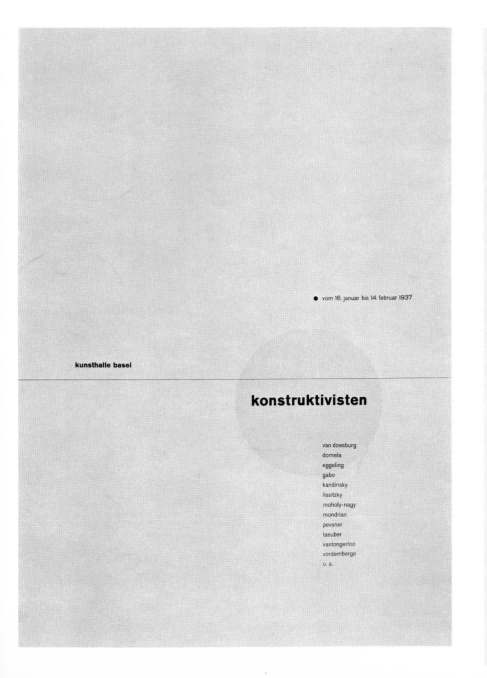

Hans Erni (Swiss, born 1909).

Atomkrieg Nein (Atom War No). 1954.
Offset lithograph, 50 x 35¼ inches.
Gift of the designer.

Karl Gerstner (Swiss, born 1930).

Auch Du bist liberal (You too are Liberal). 1959.
Offset lithograph, 50¼ x 35¼ inches.
Gift of the designer.

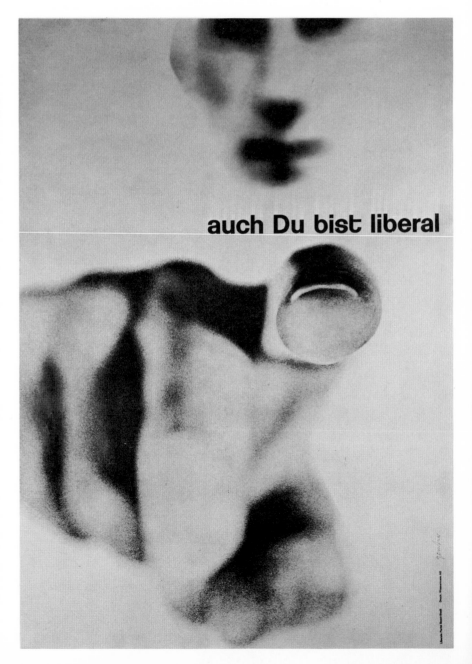

Peter Hajnoczky (Swiss, born 1943).

Winter Hilfe '62. (Winter Aid '62). 1962.
Offset lithograph, 50¼ x 35½ inches.
Anonymous gift.

Carlo Vivarelli (Swiss, born 1919).

Pour la Vieillesse Don Volontaire (For Old Age Voluntary Gift). 1949.
Offset lithograph, 50½ x 35¼ inches.
Gift of the Swiss Government.

Peter Hajnoczky (Swiss, born 1943).

Winter Hilfe '62. (Winter Aid '62). 1962.

Carlo Vivarelli (Swiss, born 1919).

Pour la Vieillesse Don Volontaire (For Old Age Voluntary Gift). 1949.

Josef Müller-Brockmann (Swiss, born 1914), designer;
Ernst Albert Heiniger (Swiss, born 1909), photographer.

Schützt das Kind! (Protect the Children!) 1958.
Offset lithograph, 50⅜ x 35⅝ inches.
Gift of the designer.

Josef Müller-Brockmann.

Der Film. 1960.
Offset lithograph, 50¼ x 35½ inches.
Gift of Kunstgewerbemuseum, Zurich.

Richard P. Lohse (Swiss, born 1902), designer;
Marlene Gruber (Swiss), photographer.

Ausstellung Musikinstrumente Kunstgewerbemuseum Zurich. 1962.
Offset lithograph, 50⅛ x 35¼ inches.
Gift of Kunstgewerbemuseum, Zurich.

Armin Hofmann (Swiss, born 1920).

Stadt Theatre Basel. 1964.
Offset lithograph, 50¼ x 35½ inches.
Gift of the designer.

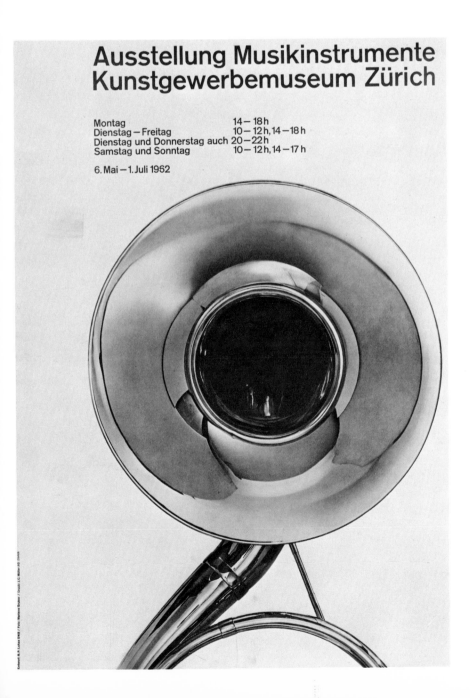

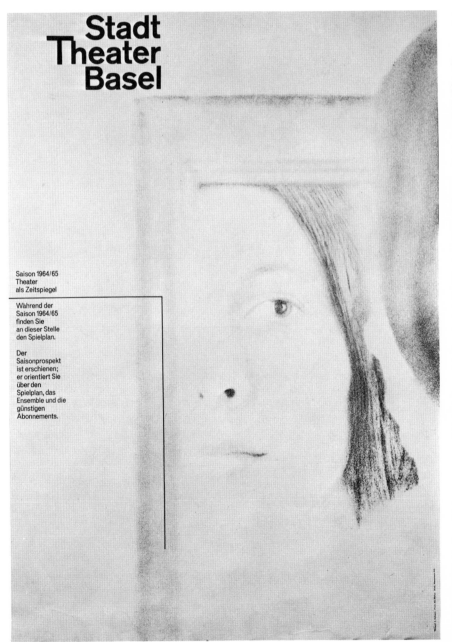

Pieter Brattinga (Dutch, born 1931).

P.T.T. de Man Achter de Vormgeving van de P.T.T. (The Man behind the
Designing of the Post and Telegraph). 1960.
Offset lithograph, 25 x 14¾ inches.
Gift of De Jong & Company.

Otto Treumann (Dutch, born Germany, 1919).

Chanoeka Joodse Feestdagen in het Joods Historisch Museum Amsterdam
(Chanuka Jewish Festival in the Jewish Historical Museum). 1963.
Offset lithograph, 19¾ x 27¼ inches.
Gift of the designer.

Fritz Fischer-Nosbisch (German, born 1919).

Apokalyptische Visionen. 1963.
Offset lithograph, 32¾ x 23½ inches.
Gift of Hessisches Landesmuseum Darmstadt.

Massimo Vignelli (Italian, born 1931; lives in U.S.A.).

31B XXXI Biennale Internazionale d'Arte. 1962.
Offset lithograph, 38½ x 26¾ inches.
Gift of the designer.

Hans Jurgen Spohn (German, born 1934).

Jugend Veranstaltungen Der XIV Internationalen Filmfestspiele Berlin (Youth
Films at the XIV International Film Festival). 1964.
Offset lithograph, 24¾ x 33 inches.
Gift of the designer.

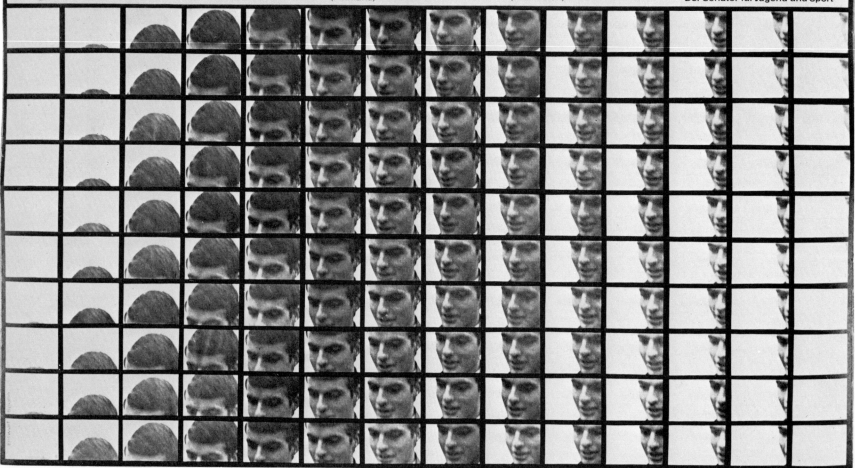

Robert Gretczko (American, born 1944) and
Charles Zimmerman (American, born 1942).

Our Town 1970. 1964.
Offset lithograph, 27⅞ x 18 inches.
Gift of the Municipal Art Society.

Wolfgang Schmidt (German, born 1930).

Schreib Galerie Gunar Düsseldorf. 1965.
Silk screen, 35 x 24 inches.
Gift of the designer.

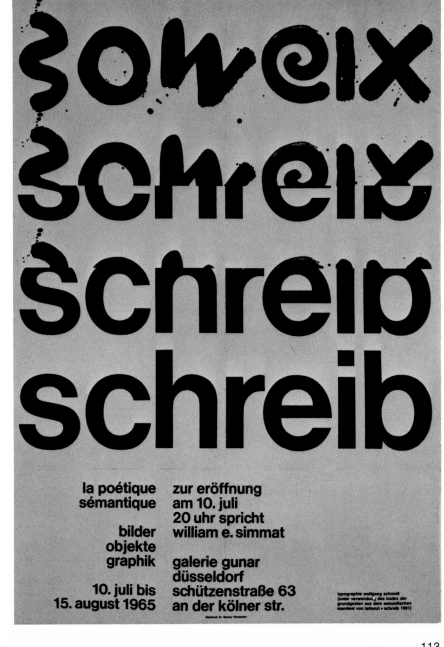

Bruno Munari (Italian, born 1907).

Campari. 1965.
Offset lithograph, 6 feet 5¼ inches x 9 feet 1¼ inches.
Gift of the designer.

Eduardo Paolozzi (British, born 1924).

Universal Electronic Vacuum 1967.
Silk screen and offset lithograph, 37¾ x 24¾ inches.
Gift of the Pace Gallery.

Wim Crouwel (Dutch, born 1928).

Vorm Gevers (Form Givers). 1968.
Offset lithograph, 39 x 26½ inches.
Gift of the designer.

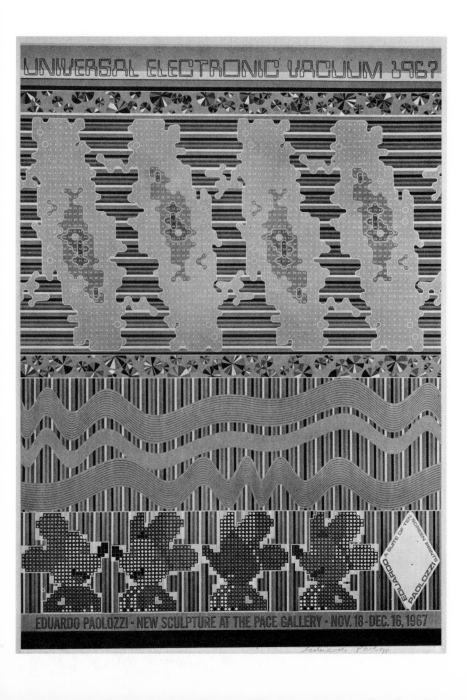

Ivan Chermayeff (American, born 1932) and
Thomas Geismar (American, born 1931).

American Graphics. 1964.
Offset lithograph, 33 x 24 inches.
Acquired by exchange.

Cristos Gianakos (American, born 1934).

Send Our Boys Home. 1966.
Offset lithograph, 12¼ x 17 inches.
Gift of the designer.

Peter Gee (English, born 1932).

Color Image. 1966.
Silk screen on aluminized paper, 21¾ x 21½ inches.
Gift of the designer.

Tomoko Miho (American, born 1931).

Great Architecture in Chicago. 1967.
Silk screen on aluminized paper, 50 x 35 inches.
Gift of Container Corporation of America.

Almir Mavignier (Brazilian, born 1925; lives in Germany).

Getulio. 1962.
Silk screen, 33¼ x 23⅜ inches.
Gift of the designer.

Johannes Reyn (German, born 1935, lives in U.S.A.).

IBM Rev-up. 1967.
Silk screen, 34¾ x 24¾ inches.
Gift of Roberts and Reyn, Inc.

Eduardo Terrazas (Mexican, born 1936) and
Lance Wyman (American, born 1937).

Mexico 68. 1967.
Offset lithograph, 35 x 34 inches.
Gift of the Organizing Committee for the XIX Olympics.

Massimo Vignelli.

Studio Verde Convegno. 1964.
Offset lithograph, 55 x 38¼ inches.
Gift of the designer.

Günther Kieser (German, born 1920).

Jazz Band Ball. 1963.
Offset lithograph, 33⅛ x 23¼ inches.
Gift of the designer.

Milton Glaser (American, born 1929).

Mahalia Jackson. 1967.
Offset lithograph, two sheets, each 38 x 24⅝ inches.
Gift of the designer.

Marisol (Marisol Escobar; Venezuelan, born France, 1930; lives in U.S.A.).

Paris Review. 1967.
Silk screen, 26 x 32½ inches.
Gift of Page, Arbitrio & Resen.

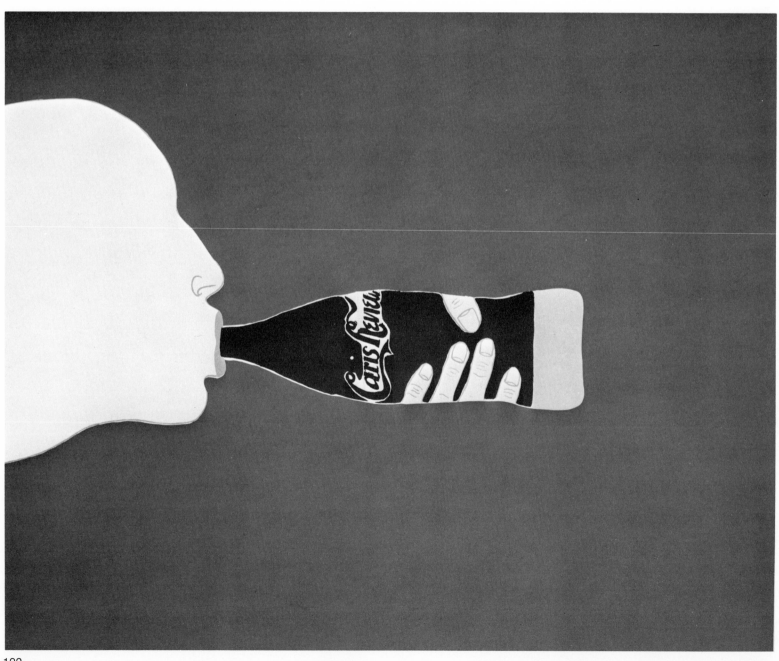

Michael English (British).

Love Festival. 1967.
Silk screen, 29⅞ x 40 inches.
Gift of P. Reyner Banham.

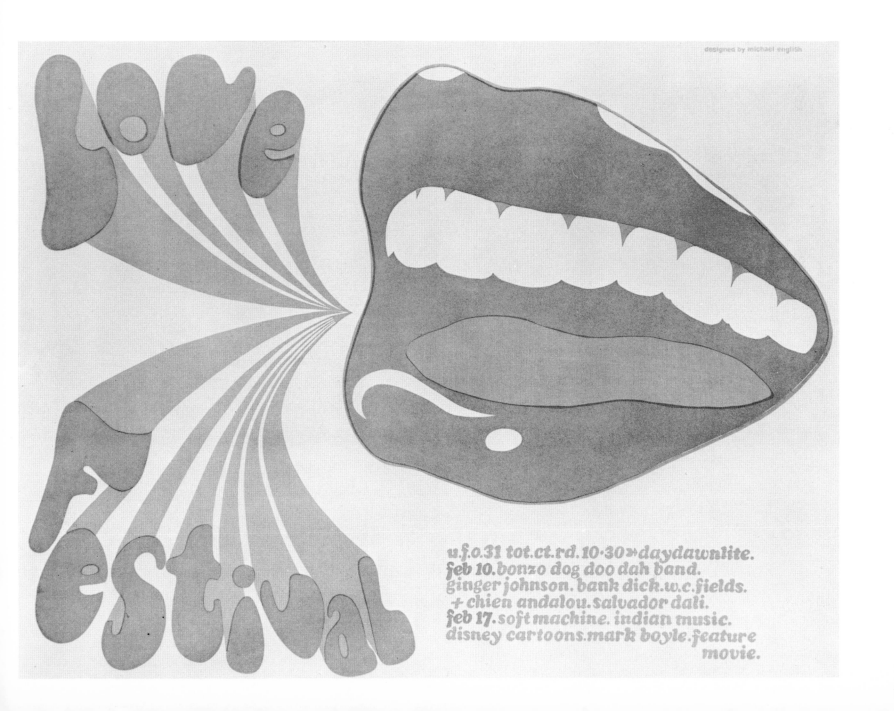

Robert Wesley Wilson (American, born 1937).

The Association. 1966.
Offset lithograph, 19⅝ x 13¾ inches.
Purchase fund.

C.H. Johansen.

Visions. 1967.
Offset lithograph, 35 x 23 inches.
Gift of Joseph H. Heil.

Victor Moscoso (American, born Spain, 1936).

Junior Wells and His Chicago Blues Band. 1966.
Offset lithograph, 19¾ x 14 inches.
Gift of the designer.

Victor Moscoso.

Hawaii Pop Rock Festival. 1967.
Offset lithograph, 20¼ x 14 inches.
Gift of the designer.

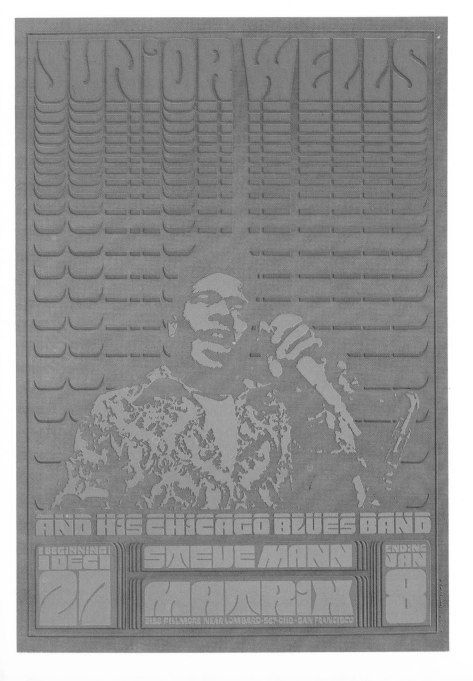

Peter Max (American, born Germany, 1937).

123 Infinity The Contemporaries. 1967.
Offset lithograph, 24 x 18⅛ inches.
Gift of the Contemporaries Gallery.

Tadanori Yokoo (Japanese, born 1936).

Made in Japan Tadanori Yokoo. 1965.
Silk screen, 43 x 31⅛ inches.
Gift of the designer.

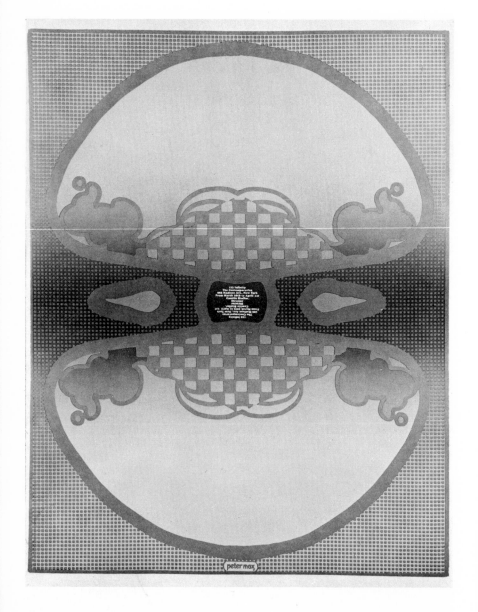

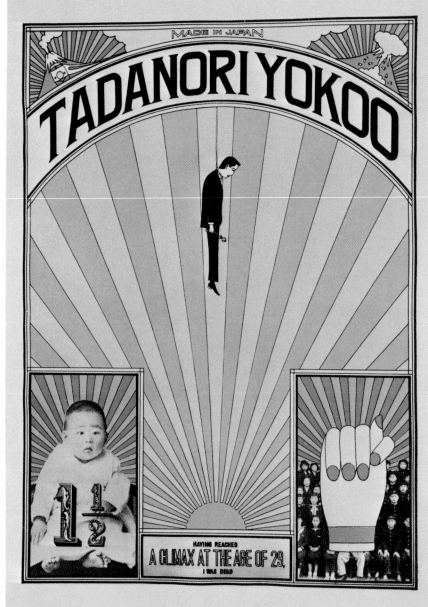

Tadanori Yokoo.

Koshimaki Osen (advertisement for a happening). 1966.
Silk screen, 41½ x 29⅜ inches.
Gift of the designer.

Tadanori Yokoo.

The City and Design Isamu Kurita. 1966.
Silk screen, 41 x 29½ inches.
Gift of the designer.

Marc Chagall (French, born Russia, 1887).

Bible Marc Chagall Verve 33-34 Editions Verve—Paris. 1956.
Lithograph, 25 x 16¼ inches.
Gift of Mourlot Frères.

Georges Braque (French, 1882 –1963).

G. Braque Galerie Maeght. 1956.
Offset lithograph, 29½ x 20¼ inches.
Gift of Mr. and Mrs. Leo W. Farland.

Pablo Picasso (Spanish, born 1881; lives in France).

Toros En Vallauris 1955.
Linoleum cut, 29½ x 20¼ inches.
Gift of Mr. and Mrs. Leo W. Farland.

Pablo Picasso.

Exposition Vallauris 1952.
Linoleum cut, 26¼ x 20¼ inches.
Gift of Curt Valentin.

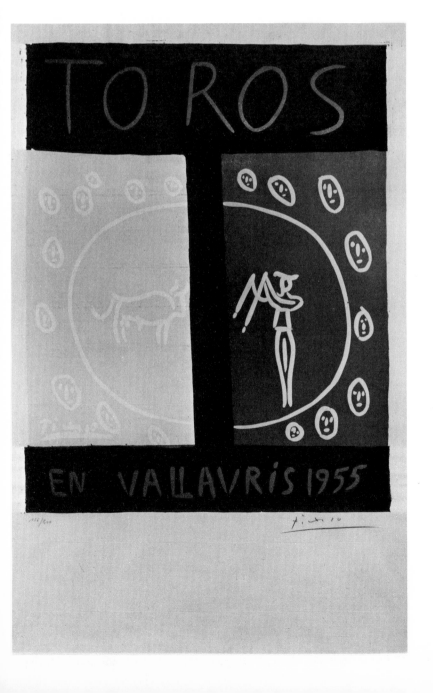

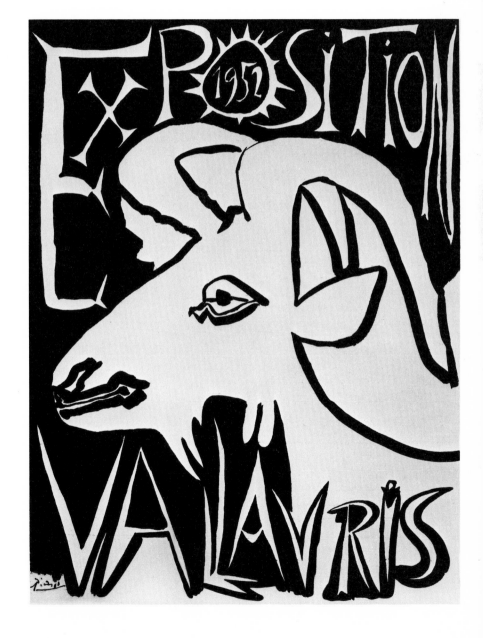

Pablo Picasso.

''Les Ménines'' Galerie Louise Leiris. 1959.
Lithograph, 26⅜ x 18¾ inches.
Gift of Mourlot Frères.

Joan Miró (Spanish, born 1893).

Miró Galerie Maeght Art Sculptures Graphique. 1950.
Lithograph, 25¾ x 19 inches.
Anonymous gift.

Le Corbusier (Charles-Edouard Jenneret; French, born Switzerland, 1887–1965).

Le Corbusier Poème de l'Angle Droit. 1955.
Lithograph, 24½ x 15⅝ inches.
Gift of Berggruen & Cie.

Fernand Léger (French, 1881–1955).

F. Léger Museum Morsbroich Leverkusen. 1955.
Lithograph, 30 x 22¼ inches.
Gift of Mourlot Frères.

Winfred Gaul (Austrian, born 1928).

Images Meditatives Ausstellung Galerie St. Stephen Wien (Meditative Images).
1960.
Silk screen, 27⅝ x 19⅝ inches.
Gift of the designer.

Jean Tinguely (Swiss, born 1925; lives in France).

Machines Tinguely for Galerie Iolas. 1966.
Lithograph, 27½ x 19 inches.
Gift of Mr. and Mrs. Leo W. Farland.

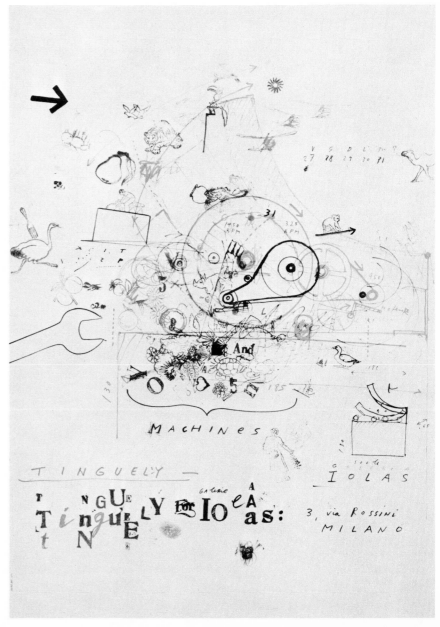

Jasper Johns (American, born 1930).

Jasper Johns Peintures & Sculptures & Dessins & Lithos. 1960.
Offset lithograph, 29¼ x 18¼ inches.
Gift of the designer.

Willem de Kooning (American, born The Netherlands, 1904).

de Kooning. 1965.
Offset lithograph, 29 x 20 inches.
Gift of the Aspen Institute for Humanistic Studies.

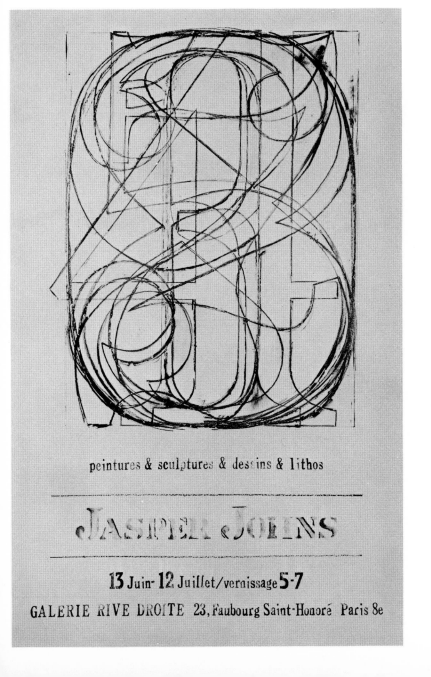

Roy Lichtenstein (American, born 1923).

Aspen Winter Jazz. 1967.
Silk screen, 40 x 26 inches.
Gift of Mr. and Mrs. Armand Bartos.

Nicholas Krushenick (American, born 1929).

American Ballet Theatre. 1968.
Offset lithograph, 84½ x 41½ inches.
Gift of List Art Posters.

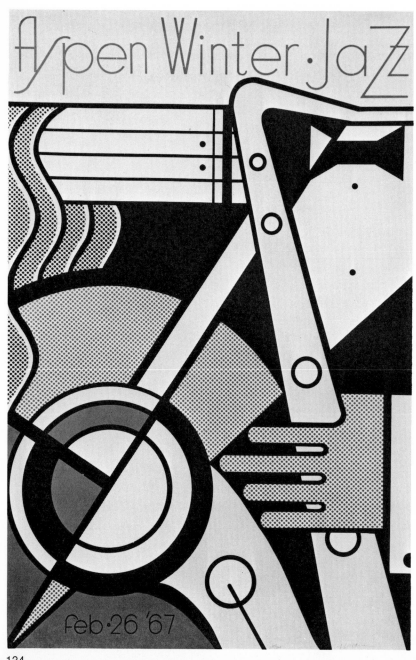

Frank Stella (American, born 1936).

Lincoln Center Festival '67.
Offset lithograph on graph paper. 44¾ x 20½ inches.
Gift of List Art Posters.

Robert Indiana (American, born 1928).

Robert Indiana New Art. 1964.
Offset lithograph, 45½ x 30¾ inches.
Gift of the designer.

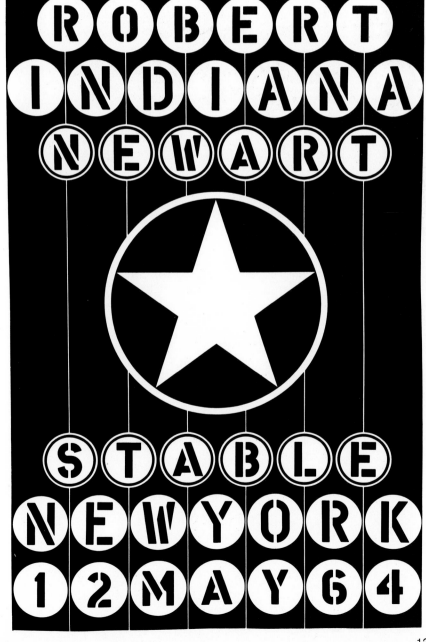

Ernest Trova (American, born 1927).

Ernest Trova Recent Sculpture. 1967.
Silk screen, 25⅞ x 26⅜ inches.
Gift of Pace Gallery.

Emilio Ambasz (Argentinian, born 1941).

Geigy Graphics on Exhibition April 1967.
Offset lithograph with die cut, 15½ x 15 inches.
Gift of the designer.

Bob Cato (American, born 1923).

Public Sculptures in Public Places. 1967.
Offset lithograph, 15¾ inches high x 25¼ inches wide at bottom x 16¾ inches wide at top.
Gift of the designer.

Andy Warhol (American, born 1930).

Paris Review. 1967.
Silk screen, 37⅛ x 27⅛ inches.
Gift of Page, Arbitrio & Resen.

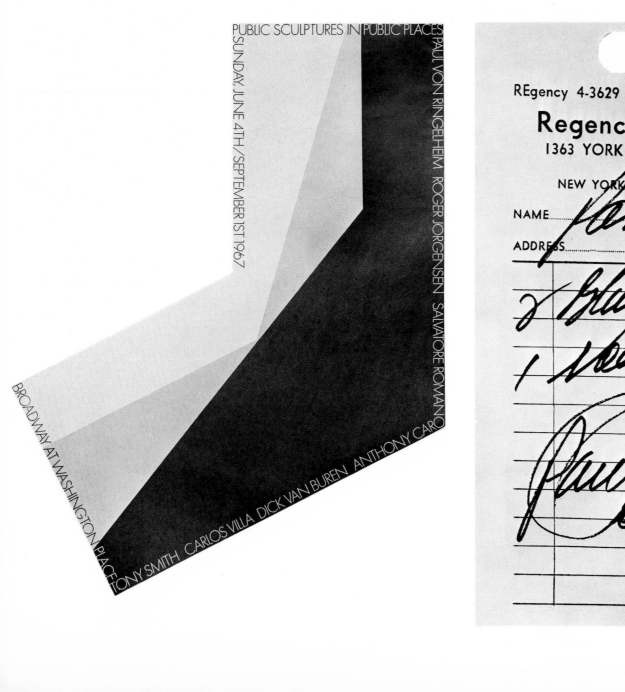

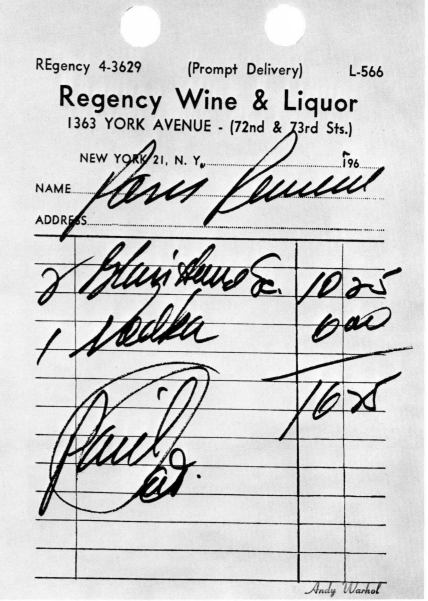

Jean Dubuffet (French, born 1901).

J. Dubuffet Ustensiles Demeures Escaliers. 1967.
Offset lithograph, 22¼ x 14¼ inches.
Gift of Galerie Jean Bucher.

Notes

1 Quoted in Arsène Alexandre, M. H. Spielmann, H. C. Bunner, and August Jaccaci, *The Modern Poster* (New York: Charles Scribner's Sons, 1895), p. 39.

2 Edgar Breitenbach, in *The American Poster* (New York: The American Federation of Arts and October House, 1967), pp. 7–20.

3 Breitenbach, *loc. cit.;* Ernest Maindron, *Les Affiches illustrées (1886–1895)* (Paris: G. Boudet, 1896), especially pp. 189–192; and Octave Uzanne, *La Nouvelle Bibliopolis* (Paris: Henri Floury, 1897), pp. 112–113.

4 Alois Senefelder, *The Invention of Lithography,* translated by J. W. Muller (New York: Fuchs and Lang Manufacturing Company, 1911), pp. 197–198. Originally published in 1817.

5 Ruari McLean, *Victorian Book Design and Colour Printing* (London: Faber and Faber; New York: Oxford University Press, 1963), pp. 25–33, 100–101, and elsewhere.

6 Maindron, *op. cit.;* and Robert J. Goldwater, '' 'L'Affiche Moderne': A Revival of Poster Art after 1880,'' *Gazette des Beaux-Arts* (Paris), December 1942, pp. 173–182.

7 Ernest Maindron, *Les Affiches illustrées* (Paris: H. Launette, 1886). Compilation of articles originally published in 1884.

8 Robert Koch, ''A Poster by Fernand Khnopff,'' *Marsyas* (New York), vol. 6, 1950–1953, pp. 72–74.

9 John Rewald, *Pierre Bonnard* (New York: The Museum of Modern Art, 1948), pp. 16, 135.

10 Octave Uzanne, ''La Monomanie des affiches,'' *op. cit.,* pp. 83–179.

11 This happened first in Brussels, where Chéret was invited to show at *Les XX,* along with avant-garde painters from France, Holland, England, and Belgium. Koch, *op. cit.;* and Bruce Laughton, ''The British and American Contribution to Les XX, 1884–93,'' *Apollo* (London) November 1967, pp. 372–379.

12 Peter Selz and Mildred Constantine, eds. (with an essay on graphic design by Alan M. Fern), *Art Nouveau* (New York: The Museum of Modern Art, 1960). *See also works* by Robert Schmutzler, Stefan Tschudi Madsen, and Mario Amaya cited in the bibliography.

13 Abraham M. Hammacher, *Le Monde de Henry van de Velde* (Antwerp: Edition Fonds Mercator; Paris: Librairie Hachette, 1967); *Henry van de Velde, 1863–1957* (Brussels: Palais des Beaux-Arts, 1963); and Henry van de Velde, *Geschichte Meines Lebens,* Hans Curjel, ed. (Munich; R. Riper, 1962).

14 Roswitha Riegger-Baurmann, ''Schrift im Jugendstil,'' *Börsenblatt für den deutschen Buchhandel* (Frankfurter Ausgabe), April 21, 1958, pp. 495–497; and Selz and Constantine, eds., *op. cit.,* p. 28.

15 Laughton, *op. cit.,* p. 376.

16 Alexandre, et al., *The Modern Poster,* p. 57.

17 *Ibid.,* p. 65.

18 There is a striking similarity between Penfield's 1897 poster for *Harper's* and Bonnard's famous four-panel screen, painted in 1892–1894. Penfield probably never saw the screen itself, but motifs from it appeared during the nineties in Bonnard lithographs that may have crossed the ocean.

19 Helen Farr Sloan, *The Poster Period of John Sloan* (Lock Haven, Pennsylvania: Hammermill Paper Company, 1967).

20 Paul Wember, *Die Jugend der Plakate, 1887–1917* (Krefeld, Germany: Richard Scherpe, [1961]).

21 First noted by G. W. Ovink, in lectures delivered in New York and Washington, 1967.

22 Quoted in Herschel B. Chipp, ed., *Jugendstil & Expressionism in German Posters* (Berkeley, California: University Art Gallery, 1965), p. 8.

23 Martin Hardie and Arthur K. Sabin, eds., *War Posters Issued by Belligerent and Neutral Nations 1914–1919* (London: A. & C. Black, 1920).

24 Jan Tschichold, *Asymmetric Typography* (New York: Reinhold Publishing Company, 1967), p. 84; translated by Ruari McLean from *Typographische Gestaltung* (Basel: Benno Schwabe, 1935).

25 *Bauhaus: Idée—Form—Zweck—Zeit* (Frankfurt-am-Main: Göppinger Galerie, 1964), pp. 62–64.

26 William S. Rubin, *Dada, Surrealism, and Their Heritage* (New York: The Museum of Modern Art, 1968) pp. 10, 42–44, 54, 96 and elsewhere.

27 Rubin, *op. cit.,* p. 34.

28 Peter Selz, "John Heartfield's Photomontages," *Massachusetts Review* (Amherst), Winter 1963, pp. 306–336; and Wieland Herzfelde, *John Heartfield* (Dresden: VEB Verlag der Kunst, 1962).

29 Helmut and Alison Gernsheim, *Creative Photography: Aesthetic Trends 1839–1860* (London: Faber and Faber, 1962), p. 195.

30 Beaumont Newhall, *The History of Photography,* rev. edition (New York: The Museum of Modern Art, 1964), p. 162.

31 Selz, *Massachusetts Review,* p. 24.

32 James Laver, Harold F. Hutchison, and Thomas E. Griffits, *Art for All: London Transport Posters, 1908–1949* (London: Art and Technics, 1949), p. 22.

33 P. M. Handover, *Grotesque Letters: A History of Unseriffed Type Faces from 1816 to the Present Day* (London: Monotype Corporation, Ltd., 1964. This is a special issue of *Monotype Newsletter* [London], number 69, 1964).

34 Archives of the Department of Architecture and Design, The Museum of Modern Art, New York; and *Posters by E. McKnight Kauffer* (New York: The Museum of Modern Art, 1937).

35 André Salmon, preface to *Maîtres Français de l'affiche* (Les Cahiers Jaunes, 3 [Paris: Librairie José Corti, 1943]), p. 15. My translation.

36 *Ibid.,* p. 7.

37 Anthony Velonis, *Technical Problems of the Artist: Technique of the Silk Screen Process* (New York: Works Progress Administration, Federal Art Project, [1938?]), 2 vol.

38 Ben Shahn, *Love and Joy about Letters* (New York: Grossman Publishers, 1963), p. 47.

39 Alan M. Fern, "Old-fashioned Types and New-fangled Typography," *Typographica 14* (London), Spring 1958, pp. 26–31.

40 Ksawery Piwocki, statement in *Polish Graphic Arts and Posters* (Warsaw: Central Office of Art Exhibitions, for Smithsonian Institution Traveling Exhibition Service, 1966).

41 *The Swiss Poster: Traveling Exhibition* (Zurich: Pro Helvetia Foundation, 1952), pp. 27–32.

42 "Olivetti: Design in Industry," *The Museum of Modern Art Bulletin* (New York), vol. XX, no. 1, Fall 1952.

Without attempting to incorporate all references cited in the many bibliographies scattered throughout the listing below, fair representation has been given to the various types of relevant materials: general works (bibl. 1–93), magazines (94–106), yearbooks (bibl. 107–110), articles (bibl. 111–137), exhibition catalogues (138–167), and various material concerning individual artists (bibl. 168–240). Considerable information, particularly biographical, will be found by using the periodical indexes, most especially *The Art Index* (New York, H. W. Wilson Co., 1929–current).

Bernard Karpel
Librarian of the Museum

1　*L'Affiche illustré: Collection Commoedia-Charpentier.*
　Paris: Les Publications Techniques et Artistiques, 1944. 36 pp., illus.
　Texts by A. M. Cassandre, Paul Colin, Jean Picart Le Doux, Maximilien
　Gauthier, Louis Cheronnet, Pierre du Colombier, and René Chavance.

2　Alexandre, Arsène and others. *The Modern Poster* by Arsène Alexandre,
　M. H. Spielmann, H. C. Bunner, and August Jaccaci.
　New York: Charles Scribner's Sons, 1895. 117 pp., illus.

3　Allner, Walter H. *Posters.*
　New York: Reinhold Publishing Corporation, 1952. 119 pp., illus.
　Fifty artists and designers analyze their approach.

　See also bibl. 108

4　Amaya, Mario. *Art Nouveau.*
　London: Studio Vista; New York: E. P. Dutton, 1966. 168 pp., illus.

5　Arnold, Friedrich. *Anschläge: Deutsche Plakate als Dokumente der Zeit
　1900–1960.*
　Ebenhausen bei Munich: Langeweische-Brandt, 1963. 122 pp., illus.
　Printed on colored papers similar to originals.

6　*Art News* (New York). Aug.–Sept. 1942, illus.
　Special issue: "First complete survey anywhere of war posters." Articles by
　Alfred M. Frankfurter, Doris Brian, C. D. McCormick, and Duncan Phillips.

7　*Art Present* (Paris). no. 4–5, 1947, illus.
　Special issue: "Présence de la publicité." Section on "Esthétique de la
　publicité," including "Optique" by Vasarely.

8　*L'Arte Moderna, Vol. 1: Realità e Forma nel Postimpressionismo.*
　Milan: Fratelli Fabbri Editori, 1967. pp. 301–320, illus.

9　Auriol, Georges. [*Livres des monogrammes*, etc.].
　Paris, 1901–1924. 3 vols., illus.
　Le premier livre des cachets, marques et monogrammes, Paris: Librairie
　Centrale des Beaux Arts, 1901. *Le seconde livre des monogrammes,
　marques, cachets et ex-libris*, Paris: Henri Floury, 1908. *Le troisième livre des
　monogrammes, cachets, marques et ex-libris*, Paris: Henri Floury, 1924.

10 Barr, Alfred H., Jr. *Cubism and Abstract Art*.
New York: The Museum of Modern Art, 1936. 249 pp., illus.
Includes posters and typography. Reprint, New York: Arno Press, 1966.

11 _____. *Masters of Modern Art*.
New York: The Museum of Modern Art, 1954. pp. 228–230, illus.

12 *Bauhausbücher*. Munich: Langen, 1925–1929. 14 vol., illus.
Possibly the most influential series on design published in modern times.
Includes texts by Mondrian (no. 5), van Doesburg (no. 6), Moholy-Nagy
(no. 8 and no. 14), Kandinsky (no. 9), and Malevich (no. 11). Several
available in other language and reprint editions; details in bibl. 10

13 Bauwens, M. and others. *Les Affiches étrangères illustrées* by M.
Bauwens, T. Hayashi, La Forgue, Meier-Graefe, J. Pennell.
Paris: Boudet, 1897. 206 pp., illus.

14 Bayer, Herbert, Walter Gropius, and Ise Gropius, eds. *Bauhaus 1919–1928*.
Boston: Charles T. Branford Co., 1959. 224 pp., illus., bibl.
First edition, New York: The Museum of Modern Art, 1938. Second printing,
1952; third, 1959. Chronology, biographical notes.

15 Beraldi, Henri. *Les Graveurs du XIXième Siècle*.
Paris: 1885–1892. v.4, pp. 168–203.
Lists Chéret's works.

Binder, Joseph. See bibl. 174

16 Brattinga, Pieter, Jr. and Dick Dooijes. *A History of the Dutch Poster,
1890–1966*.
Amsterdam: Scheltema & Holkema (In preparation, 1968). [170] pp., illus.
Preface by H. L. C. Jaffé.

17 Cassou, Jean, Emil Langui, and Nikolaus Pevsner. *Gateway to the
Twentieth Century*.
New York: McGraw-Hill Book Company, 1962. 362 pp., illus., incl. 52 plates.

18 Constantine, Mildred. *Lettering by Modern Artists*.
New York: The Museum of Modern Art, 1964. 35 pp., illus.
Based on exhibition *Lettering by Hand* prepared 1962, expanded 1963.

See also bibl. 112, 113, 154, 155, 231

19 Crane, Walter. *William Morris to Whistler*.
London: Bell, 1911. 277 pp., illus.

20 Damase, Jacques. *Révolution typographique depuis Stéphane Mallarmé*.
Geneva: Galerie Motte, 1966. [38] pp., illus., bibl.

21 Delevoy, Robert L. *Dimensions of the 20th Century*.
[Lausanne, etc.]: Editions d'Art Skira, 1965. 223 pp., illus.
Includes ''The World of the Poster,'' pp. 27–34, and scattered references,
pp. 15–16 et passim.

See also bibl. 235

22 Demeure de Beaumont, A. *L'Affiche illustré. I: L'Affiche belge*.
Toulouse: Chez l'Auteur, 1897. [130] pp., illus. Biographies.

23 Eckersley, Tom. *Poster Design*.
London and New York: The Studio, 1954. 96 pp., illus.

Fern, Alan M. See bibl. 154, 220

24 Gasser, Manuel. *Exempla Graphica*.
Zurich: Hug and Söhne, [1968?]. 175 pp., illus.
''Case histories of seventy eight works by seventy eight members of the
Alliance Graphique Internationale.'' Brief biographies.

25 Gernsheim, Helmut. *The History of Photography*.
London and New York: Oxford University Press, 1955. 395 pp., illus.
Written in collaboration with Alison Gernsheim. An exhibition from the
Gernsheim collection.

26 _____ and Alison Gernsheim. *Creative Photography: 1826 to the Present*.
Detroit: Wayne State University Press; Toronto: Ambassador Books, Ltd.,
1963. 130 pp., illus.

27 Grüningen, Berchtold von. *Vom Impressionismus zum Tachismus:
Malerei, Lithographie, Photographie, angewandte Graphik*.
Basel: Birkhäuser, 1964. 280 pp., illus., bibl.

28 Guerrand, Roger H. *L'Art Nouveau en Europe.*
Paris: Plon, 1965. 237 pp., illus.
Preface by Aragon, "Le 'Modern Style' d'où je suis," pp. vii–xxxi.

29 Handover, P. M. *Grotesque Letters: A History of Unseriffed Type Faces from 1816 to the Present Day.*
London: Monotoype Corporation Ltd., 1964. (A special issue of *Monotype Newsletter,* 69).

30 Hardie, Martin and Arthur K. Sabin, eds. *War Posters Issued by Belligerent and Neutral Nations 1914–1919.*
London: A. F. & C. Black, 1920. 46 pp., illus.

31 Herdeg, Walter, ed. *Photographis '68. International Annual of Advertising Photography.*
Zurich: The Graphis Press; New York: Hastings House, 1968. 274 pp., illus.
Includes poster section. Text in English, French, and German.

See also bibl. 107

32 Hiatt, Charles. *Picture Posters.*
London: George Bell, 1895. 367 pp., illus.

33 *Jugendstil—Art Nouveau. Buchkunst um 1900.—Plakate—Graphik—Glaser.*
Berne, Kornfeld und Klipstein; Zurich, L'Art Ancien: 1968. 156 pp., plus 27 plates.
Comprehensive annotated catalogue for auction 124 held in Berne at Kornfeld und Klipstein.

34 Klingspor, Karl. *Uber Schönheit von Schrift und Druck.*
Frankfurt-am-Main: Schauer, 1949. 155 pp., illus.

35 Kowalski, Tadeusz. *Polski Plakat Filmowy.*
Warsaw: Filmowa Agencja Wydawnicza, 1957. 142 pp., illus.
Text in Polish, French, Russian, English, and German.

36 Laver, James. *XIXth Century French Posters.*
London: Nicholson & Watson, 1944. 18 pp. plus 25 plates.
Preface by Henry Davray. Based on exhibition at Leicester Galleries.

37 _____and others. *Art For All: London Transport Posters 1908–1949,* by James Laver, Harold F. Hutchison, and Thomas E. Griffits.
London: Art and Technics, 1949. 33 pp. plus 68 plates.

38 Lo Duca, Guiseppe. *L'Affiche.*
Paris: Presses Universitaires de France, 1945. 127 pp., illus., bibl.

39 Madsen, Stephan Tschudi. *Art Nouveau.*
New York, Toronto: McGraw-Hill Book Company, 1967. 256 pp., illus. (World University Library).

40 _____. *Sources of Art Nouveau.*
New York: George Wittenborn; Oslo: H. Aschehoug. [1955]. 488 pp., illus., bibl.

41 Maindron, Ernest. *Les Affiches illustrées.*
Paris: H. Launette, 1886. 160 pp., illus., plus 30 plates.
With essays first published 1884.

42 _____. *Les Affiches illustrées, 1886–1895.*
Paris: G. Boudet, 1896. 251 pp., illus., plus 64 plates.

43 *Les Maîtres de l'Affiche.*
Paris: L'Imprimerie Chaix, 1896–1900. 5 folio vols., illus.
Prefaces by M. Roger-Marx.

44 *Maîtres français de l'Affiche: Jean Carlu, A. M. Cassandre, Paul Colin, Charles Loupot, Germaine Mary.*
Paris: Librairie José Corti, 1943. 42 pp., illus. (Les Cahiers jaunes, 3).
Preface by André Salmon.

45 Marx, Roger. "Le Musée de l'affiche," *L'Art social.*
Paris: E. Fasquelle, 1913, pp. 104–107.

46 Mascha, Ottokar. *Osterreichische Plakatkunst.*
Vienna: J. Löwy, 1915. 8 pp. plus 124 plates.

47 McLean, Ruari. *Victorian Book Design and Colour Printing.*
London: Faber and Faber; New York: Oxford University Press, 1963. 182 pp., illus.

48 Metzl, Ervine. *The Poster: Its History and Its Art.*
New York: Watson-Guptill, 1963. 183 pp., illus.

49 Milan. Ente Manifestazioni Milanesi. *Il Manifesto Italiano.*
Milan: Società per le Belle Arti e Esposizione Permanente, 1965. 55 pp., illus.
Essays by A. M. Brizio and A. Rossi.

50 *Monographien deutscher Reklamekünstler.*
Hagen. Deutscher Museum für Kunst in Handel und Gewerbe and
F. W. Ruhfus, 1911–1914. 7 vol.
Vol. 1–2, F. H. and Clara Ehmcke; 3, Julius Klinger; 4, Lucian Bernhard;
5, Peter Behrens; 6, Gipkens; 7, Emil Preetorius.

51 Mourlot, Fernand. *Art in Posters: The Complete Original Posters of Braque,
Chagall, Dufy, Léger, Matisse, Miró, Picasso.*
Monte Carlo: André Sauret; New York: George Braziller, 1959. 247 pp.,
102 color plates, and checklist.

52 Mroszczak, Józef. *Polnische Plakatkunst.*
Vienna, Düsseldorf: Econ, 1962. [20] pp., illus.

See also bibl: 162

53 *Museum of Modern Art Bulletin* (New York). v. 20, no. 1, 1952.
Special issue: "Olivetti: design in industry."

54 Neumann, Eckhard. *Functional Graphic Design in the 20's.*
New York: Reinhold Publishing Corp., 1967. 96 pp., illus.
Includes Walter Dexel: "What is New Typography?" in German and English,
pp. 54–63. (Originally published *Frankfurter Zeitung*
[Frankfurt-am-Main], Feb. 5, 1927).

See also bibl. 126, 144

55 _____and Wolfgang Sprang, eds. *Werbung in Deutchland, Jahrbuch der
deutsche Werbung.*
Düsseldorf, Vienna: Econ, 1964.
Advertising of manufacturers, arranged by type.

56 Newhall, Beaumont. *The History of Photography* (rev. ed.).
New York, The Museum of Modern Art, 1964. 212 pp., illus., bibl.

57 New York Public Library, Art Division. *[Poster albums assembled by artists.]*
New York, 1893–1924. 10 vol.
Atlas folios of mounted and bound examples, arranged alphabetically. Highly
variable in quality, reflecting commercial usage of three decades.

Niggli, Arthur. See bibl. 113

58 Pevsner, Nikolaus. *Pioneers of Modern Design: From William Morris to
Walter Gropius.*
New York: The Museum of Modern Art, 1949. 253 pp., illus.
Revised version of British edition, London: Faber and Faber, 1936.

59 Pica, Vittorio. *Attraverso gli Albi e le Cartelle: Serie 1–3.*
Bergamo: Istituto Italiano d'Arti Grafiche, 1902–1916. illus.

60 *Plakate der Russischen Revolution, 1917–1929.*
Berlin: Gerhardt, 1966. [12] pp., plus 40 plates in folio.
Preface and captions by Giuseppe Garritano. See also bibl. 73

61 Polak, Bettina. *Het Fin-de-siècle in de nederlandse Schilderkunst.*
The Hague: Nijhoff, 1955. 415 pp., illus.
English summary.

62 *Das Politische Plakat.*
Charlottenburg: Verlag Das Plakat, 1919. 49 pp., plus 22 plates.
Includes "Alte und neue Plakate," by A. Behne; "Flugblatt und Flugschrift,"
by P. Landau; and "Warum sozialistische Propaganda?" by H. Löwing.

63 *Posters and Their Designers.*
London: The Studio, 1924–1929.
Special autumn numbers of *The Studio,* later to become an annual,
Modern Publicity. See bibl. 109

64 Price, Charles Matlack. *Poster Design* (new edition).
New York: G. W. Bricka, 1922. 370 pp., illus.

65 Purvis, Tom. *Poster Progress*.
London and New York: The Studio, n.d. 128 pp., illus.

Illustrations selected by F. A. Mercer and W. Gaunt.

66 Rademacher, Hellmut. *Masters of German Poster Art*.
Leipzig: Edition Leipzig, 1966. 139 pp., illus.

67 Rheims, Maurice. "Affiches," *L'Art 1900, ou le Style Jules Verne*.
Paris: Arts et Métiers Graphiques, 1965. pp. 366–380, illus.

68 Richmond, Leonard, ed. *The Technique of the Poster*.
London: I. Pitman & Sons, 1933. 207 pp., illus.
"The posters of McKnight Kauffer," pp. 167–172.

69 Rickards, Maurice. *Posters at the Turn of the Century*.
New York: Walker, 1968. 72 pp., illus.

70 _____. *Posters of the Nineteen-Twenties*.
New York: Walker, 1968. 72 pp., illus.

71 Rossi, Attilio. *I Manifesti*.
Milan: Fratelli Fabbri Editori, 1966. 158 pp., illus., bibl.

72 Ruben, Paul, ed. *Die Reklame*.
Berlin: H. Patel, 1914. 2 vol., illus.

73 *Russian Revolutionary Posters, 1917–1927*.
New York: Grove Press, 1967. [16] pp., plus 40 plates.
Research by Caio Garruba; notes by Stefan Congrat-Butlar. Otherwise identical with bibl. 60

74 Sachs, Hans J. *The World's Largest Poster Collection, 1896–1938*.
New York: Privately printed, 1957. 44 pp., illus., bibl.
The author's collection, confiscated and lost by the Nazis.

75 Sailer, Anton. *Das Plakat* (2nd edition).
Munich: Karl Thiemig, 1965. 207 pp., illus. First publ. 1963.

76 Schardt, Hermann. *Paris 1900: Französische Plakatkunst*.
Stuttgart: Christian Belser, 1968. 184 pp., incl. 72 color plates.
Lithographs from the collection of the Folkwangschule.

77 Scheidig, Walther. *Bauhaus Weimar, 1919–1924*.
[Leipzig]: Edition Leipzig, 1966. 157 pp., illus.

78 _____. *Weimar: Crafts of the Bauhaus, 1919–1924*.
New York: Reinhold Publishing Corp., 1967. 140 pp., illus.
Translated from the German edition, [Leipzig]: Edition Leipzig, 1966.

79 Schmutzler, Robert. *Art Nouveau*.
New York: Harry N. Abrams, 1964. 321 pp., illus., bibl.
Translated from the German, Stuttgart: Gerd Hatje, 1962.

80 Schockel, Erwin. *Das politische Plakat: Eine psychologische Betrachtung*.
Munich: Eigentum der NSDAP, Franz Eher Nachf., 1938. 248 pp., illus.

81 Seling Helmut. *Jugendstil, der Weg ins 20. Jahrhundert*.
Heidelberg, Munich: Keysersche Verlagsbuchhandlung, 1959.
459 pp., illus., bibl.
Introduction by Kurt Bauch, "Plakat" by Dr. Annemarie Hagnar, pp. 249–277.

82 Senefelder, Alois. *The Invention of Lithography*.
New York: Fuchs and Lang Manufacturing Co., 1911. 229 pp.
Translated by J. W. Muller. Originally published Munich, 1817.

83 Sponsel, Jean Louis. *Das moderne Plakat*.
Dresden: Gerhard Kühtmann, 1897. 316 pp., illus.

84 Szemberg, Henryk, ed. *Polish Poster*.
Warsaw: Wydawnictwo Artystyczno-Graficzno RSW "Prassa," [1957?].
188 pp., illus.

85 Tolmer, A. *Mise en Page: the Theory and Practice of Layout*.
London: The Studio, 1931. [144] pp., illus.

86 Tschanen, Armin and Walter Bangerter, eds. *Official Graphic Art in Switzerland.*
Zurich: ABC, 1964. 184 pp., illus.
Texts in German, French, and English by Hans Peter Tschudi and Werner Kämpfen.

Tschichold, Jan. See bibl. 228–230.

87 Uzanne, Octave. *La Nouvelle Bibliopolis.*
Paris: Henri Floury, 1897. 254 pp., illus.
Includes "La Monomanie des Affiches," pp. 83–179.

88 Villani, Dino. *Storia del manifesto pubblicatario.*
Milan: Omnia, 1964. 399 pp., illus.
Chapter summaries in French, English, and German.

89 Walker, Cummings C., ed. *The Great Poster Trip: Art Eureka.*
Palo Alto: Coyne & Blanchard, 1968. 79 pp., illus.
Includes psychedelic poster artists of California.

90 Weinstock, Nino. *Plakate, I–II.*
Basel: Basilius Press, 1966–1967. 2 vol., illus.
I: Jugendstil. II. Art Déco. Each boxed volume includes 8 color posters in folder. Text in German, English, and French.

91 Wember, Paul. *Die Jugend der Plakate, 1887–1917.*
Krefeld: Scherpe Verlag, 1961. 342 pp., illus., bibl.
Biographies. Includes poster collection of the Kaiser Wilhelm Museum.

92 *Who's Who in Graphic Art.* Walter Amstutz, ed.
Zurich: Amstutz & Herdeg, 1962. [654] pp., illus.

93 Zur Western, Walter von. *Reklamekunst.*
Bielefeld: Velthagen & Klasing, 1903, 2nd edition, 1914. 148 pp., illus.
(Sammlung illustrierter Monographien, 13.)

94 *Arts et Métiers Graphiques* (Paris). 1927–1939.
Periodical devoted to fine printing, advertising, design, etc.
See its "Index, 1927–1939" under "Publicité" and names of designers.

95 *Derrière le Miroir* (Paris). 1960–current.
Recent subscriptions may include posters published by Maeght, Editeur.
Yearly checklists issued since 1960.

96 *Designers in Britain.* London, Society of Industrial Designers; later Society of Industrial Artists. 1947–current.

97 *Estampe et l'Affiche: Revue d'Art* (Paris). 1897–1899.
Concerns prints and posters of nineteenth-century France.

98 *Gebrauchsgraphik—International Advertising Art (Berlin).* 1925–current.
Articles and illustrations provide representative coverage (fair to superior) of work in many graphic fields, including posters. Texts in German and English.
Indexed in *The Art Index.*

99 *Graphic Design* (Tokyo). 1960(?)–current.
Katzumie (Masaru), ed.
Includes English contents page and captions. Commercial art and design, publicity and posters, generally of superior quality.

100 *Graphis* (Zurich). 1944–current.
Probably the best of recent magazines devoted to advertising and commercial art, including posters. Texts in German, French, and English.
Regularly indexed in *The Art Index* since v. 7 (1947–1950. Also yearly anthology (bibl. 107).

101 *Neue Graphik—New Graphic Design—Graphisme actuel* (Zurich).
Richard P. Lohse, J. Müller-Brockmann, et al., eds. 1958–current.
Texts in German, English, and French. Highly selective coverage on graphic media, including posters and outstanding designers.

102 *Das Plakat* (Berlin). 1910–1921.
Also titled: *Mitteilungen des Vereins der Plakatfreunde* (1910–1912).
Supplement: *Kultur der Reklame* (1919–1921).

103 *La Plume* (Paris). Oct. 1, 1895.

Special number: "L'Affiche internationale illustré." Includes list of posters published by or available at *La Plume.* Similar coverage, e.g. 1894, pp. 475–508, etc.

104 *PM,* later *AD* (New York). 1934–1942.
P(roduction) M(anager), later *A(dvertising) D(irector).*
Representative articles: Lucian Bernhard, "What's Wrong with the American poster?" Mar. 1936, pp. 9–14; Edward McKnight Kauffer, "Advertising art now," Dec.–Jan. 1941–1942, pp. 1–16; Percy Seitlin, "American posters and Cassandre," Jan. 1937, pp. 17–22.

105 *Poster and Art Collector* (London). Vol. 1–6, 1898–1901.
Successor to *Poster* (1898–1899). Numerous articles and reproductions, international in scope.

106 *Print: A Quarterly Journal of the Graphic Arts* (New York). 1940–current.
Good presentation of graphic and commerical art including reproduction processes, posters, etc. Indexed in *The Art Index.*

107 *Graphis Annual: International Advertising Art.* Zurich: Amstutz & Herdeg, The Graphis Press, 1952–current.
Walter Herdeg and Charles Rosner, eds. Text in English, French, and German.

108 *International Poster Annual.* St. Gall and Teufen, Switzerland: Zollikofer, 1949–current.
St. Gall, 1948–1952; Teufen, 1953–to date. Editors include Walter H. Allner and Arthur Niggli. American imprint varies.

109 *Modern Publicity.* London and New York: The Studio, 1927–current.
Until 1930 titled: *Posters & Publicity.* F. A. Mercer and W. Gaunt, eds. Uneven in quality and reflecting largely commercial standards, it covers a wide range of graphic media.

110 *Penrose Annual: Review of the Graphic Arts.* London: Lund Humphries, 1895–current.
Also titled *Process Yearbook, Penrose's Pictorial Annual* (1895–1905). Covers all graphics, including posters.

111 Barman, Christian. "London Transport publicity,"
Penrose Annual (London), 1940, pp. 50–54, illus.

112 Constantine, Mildred. "The poster collection,"
Museum of Modern Art Bulletin (New York), June 1951, 16 pp., illus.
Includes chronology of 31 museum poster competitions and exhibitions
(1933–1951), p. 15.

113 _____. "Posters from Latin America"
AD (New York), no. 6, 1941, pp. 15–22, illus.

114 Dooijes, Dick "Typography for Today: Some Important Trends in Dutch
Typographical Design,"
Delta (Amsterdam), Summer 1960, pp. 16–52, illus.

115 Frenzel, Herman K. "From Utamaro to Cassandre,"
Penrose Annual (London), v. 36, 1934, pp. 1–7, illus.

116 Gauthier, E. Paul. "Lithographs of the Revue Blanche,"
Magazine of Art (New York), Oct. 1952, pp. 273–278, illus.

117 Goldwater, Robert J. " 'L'Affiche moderne': A Revival of Poster Art after
1880,"
Gazette des Beaux-Arts (Paris), Dec. 1942, pp. 173–182, illus., bibl.

See also bibl. 153

118 Hiatt, Charles, comp., "Materials for a bibliography of the poster,"
Poster and Art Collector (London), v. 1, 1898, pp. 128, 172–173, 1216;
v. 2, pp. 120, 166, 248.

119 Homar, Lorenzo. "The Puerto Rican poster,"
Artist's Proof (New York), no. 9–10, 1966, pp. 90–95, illus.

120 "The House of Mourlot,"
Lithopinion (New York), no. 10, 1968, pp. 28–48, illus.

121 Koch, Robert. "A poster by Fernand Khnopff,"
Marsyas (New York), v. 6, 1950–1953, pp. 72–74, bibl.

122 _____. "The poster movement and 'art nouveau,'"
Gazette des Beaux-Arts (Paris), Nov. 1957, pp. 285–296, illus., bibl.
Based on unpublished thesis "The Poster in the Development of the Modern
Movement, 1880–1890," New York University, Institute of Fine Arts, 1953.

123 Laughton, Bruce. "The British and American Contribution to Les XX,
1884–93,"
Apollo (London), Nov. 1967, pp. 372–379, illus.

124 Laver, James. "Great Posters of the Past,"
Strand Magazine (London), Mar. 1942, pp. 68–73, illus.

125 Majorick, Bernard. "Posters in the Netherlands,"
Delta (Amsterdam), Summer 1961, pp. 31–56, illus.

126 Neumann, Eckhard. "Typografie, Grafik und Werbung am Bauhaus,"
Neue Grafik (Zurich), Feb. 1965, pp. 29–51, illus.
Text in German, French, and English.

127 Renner, Paul. "Die Anfänge das Künstlerplakates,"
Zeitschrift für Kunst (Leipzig), no. 2, 1947, pp. 65–71, illus.

128 Riegger-Baurmann, Roswitha. "Schrift im Jugendstil,"
Börsenblatt für den deutschen Buchhandel (Frankfurt-am-Main),
April 21, 1958, pp. 483–545.
Excerpts: "Art Nouveau script," *Architectural Review* (London), June 1958,
pp. 369–372.

129 Rosenthal, Nan. "Brightening the scene: List art posters,"
Art in America (New York), Apr. 1965, pp. 56–65, illus.

130 Rotzler, Willy. "Evolution of the photographic poster,"
Camera (Lucerne), Oct. 1959, pp. 29–38, illus.

131 Sachs, Hans J. "20 Jahre deutscher Plakatkunst,"
Archiv für Buchgewerbe (Leipzig), v. 52, 1915, pp. 238–248, illus.

132 Singer, Hans W. "Plakatkunst,"
Pan (Berlin), no. 5, 1895–1896, pp. 329–336, illus.

133 Sutton, Denys. "The Revue Blanche,"
    Signature (London), no. 18, 1954, pp. 21–43, illus.

134 Wolf, Georg Jacob. "Kubismus und Plakat,"
    Das Plakat (Munich), Sept.–Nov. 1916, pp. 262–266, illus.

135 Zahar, Marcel. "L'Affiche de 1900 à 1939: Paul Colin, A.M. Cassandre,"
    Arts de France (Paris), no. 17–18, 1947, pp. 31–46, illus.

136 _____. "Mourlot: imprimeur d'affiche,"
    Publimondial (Paris), no. 48, 1953, pp. 16–27, illus.
    Text in French, German, and English.

137 Zur Western, Walter von. "Das Plakat,"
    Zeitschrift für Bücherfreunde (Leipzig), vol. 7, 1903–1904, p. 89–129;
    vol. 11, 1907–1908, pp. 1–10, illus.

138 Berkeley, California. University Art Gallery. *Jugendstil & Expressionism in German Posters*. 1965. 48 pp., illus., bibl.
    Edited by Herschel B. Chipp; chronology and catalogue
    by Brenda Richardson.

139 Bremen. Kunsthalle. *Europäischer Jugendstil . . . aus dem Besitz der Kunsthalle Bremen*. May 16–July 18, 1965. 227 pp., illus., bibl.
    "Das Plakat," pp. 72–82.

140 Brussels. Cercle "Les XX." [Catalogues]. 1884–1893. 10 vol.
    "Couverture de G. Lemmen (2 couleurs), reproduite par l'affiche de l'exposition," 1891, 1892, 1893.

141 Brussels. Musées Royaux des Beaux-Arts de Belgique. *Le Groupe des XX et son Temps*. Feb. 17–Apr. 18, 1962. 148 pp., illus., bibl.
    Introduction by A. M. Hammacher; preface by F. C. Legrand.

142 Darmstadt. Hessisches Landesmuseums. *Plakate um 1900*. Jan. 26–April 1, 1962. 80 pp., illus., bibl.
    Includes catalogue of the poster collection.

143 Fraiture-en-Condroz (Belgium). L'Association Royale des Demeures Historiques de Belgique. *Les Affiches de la Belle Epoque, Exposition*. Sept. 9–Oct. 31, 1961. 115 pp., illus., bibl.
    Preface by François Mathey. Catalogue by Yolande Wittamer.

144 Frankfurt-am-Main. Göppinger Galerie. *Werbegrafik 1920–1930; grafische, typografische, fotografische, experimente der zwanziger Jahre*. June 27–July 20, 1963. 43 pp., illus., bibl.
    Organized by Eckhard Neumann.

145 Hamburg. Museum für Kunst und Gewerbe. *Plakat und Buchkunst um 1900*. Mar. 1–May 12, 1963. 109 pp., illus.
    Preface and catalogue by Heinz Spielmann.

146 Lucerne. Kunstmuseum. *Vingt-cinq ans d'affiches parisiennes, 1880–1905*. July 9–Oct. 2, 1950. [14] pp., plus 16 plates.
    Preface by Georges Duthuit.

147 New York. The American Federation of Arts and October House. *The*

American Poster. 1967. 71 pp., illus., bibl.
Text by Edgar Breitenbach and Margaret Cogswell.
Catalogue for exhibition circulated June 1967–June 1969.

148 New York. American Heritage Publishing Co. *Posters U.S.A.: An Exhibition of American Posters from the Collection of Levi Berman.* 1957. n.p., illus.
Sponsored by American Heritage, the Detroit Historical Museum, and the American Federation of Arts.

149 New York. IBM Gallery. *The Heritage of French Poster Art.* June 21–July 19, 1966. 16 pp., illus.
Preface by René Salanon. Sponsored by Air France.

150 New York. The Museum of Modern Art. *Britain at War.* May 22–Sept. 2, 1941. pp. 86–89, illus.

151 New York. The Museum of Modern Art. *United Hemisphere Posters.* Oct. 21–Nov. 24, 1942. 16 pp., illus.
Text in Portuguese, Spanish, and English.

152 New York. The Museum of Modern Art. *Art in Progress.* May 24–Sept. 17, 1944. pp. 202–209, illus.

153 New York. The Museum of Modern Art. *Modern Art in Your Life.* 1949. 48 pp., illus.
Catalogue by Robert Goldwater and René d'Harnoncourt of exhibition illustrating relationships between ''fine'' and ''applied'' arts. Also issued as *The Bulletin of The Museum of Modern Art* (New York), vol. XVII, no. 1, 1949, and in revised edition, 1953.

154 New York. The Museum of Modern Art. *Art Nouveau: Art and Design at the Turn of the Century.* June 6–Sept. 6, 1960. 192 pp., illus., bibl.
Edited by Peter Selz and Mildred Constantine with articles by Greta Daniel, Alan M. Fern, Henry-Russell Hitchcock, and Peter Selz. Bibliography by James Grady is a revision of ''A Bibliography of the Art Nouveau,'' *Journal of the Society of Architectural Historians* (Philadelphia), v. 14, no. 2, 1955, pp. 18–27.

155 New York. The Museum of Modern Art. *The photographic poster* [news release]. Sept. 7–Oct. 31, 1964. 2 pp.

For exhibition organized by Mildred Constantine.

156 New York. The Museum of Modern Art. *Dada, Surrealism, and Their Heritage.* March 27–June 9, 1968. 252 pp., illus., bibl.
Text by William S. Rubin. Chronology by Irene Gordon.

157 Oostende. Kursaal. *Europa 1900.* 1967. 92 pp.
Publ. Brussels: Editions de la Connaissance. A separate album of plates was published.

158 Paris. Musée National d'Art Moderne. *Bonnard, Vuillard et les Nabis.* 1955. 110 pp., plus 25 plates.
Publ. Editions des Musées Nationaux.

159 Paris. Palais du Louvre. Bibliothèque des Arts Décoratifs. *Cents Ans d'Affiche: ''La Belle Epoque.''* Summer 1964. 98 pp., illus., bibl.
Catalogue by René Salanon and Claude Samson, of 368 works in the collection of the Bibliothèque.

160 Philadelphia. Franklin Institute of the State of Pennsylvania. *New Poster.* 1937. [64] pp., illus.
International exposition of design in outdoor advertising. Essays by Christian Brinton, A. M. Cassandre, and Charles T. Coiner.

161 Vienna. Bund Osterreichischer Gegrauchsgraphiker. *Osterreichische Plakate, Austrian Posters, 1890–1957.* 1957. 64 pp., illus.
Text in German, English, and French. Publ. Anton Schroll.

162 Warsaw. Bureau Central des Expositions d'Art. *Iᵉ Biennale Internationale de l'Affiche Varsovie.* 1966, n.p., illus.
Preface in Polish and French by Jósef Mroszczak.

163 Warsaw. Muzeum Lenina. *Miedzynarodoivy Plakat Revolucyjny, 1917–1967.* [1967?]. 84 pp., illus.
Brief multilingual texts, including English, on *The Exhibition of International Revolutionary Posters.* Publ. Centralne Biuro Wystaw Artyztycznch.

164 Washington, D.C. Smithsonian Institution. *Polish Graphic Arts and Posters.* 1966. n.p., illus.
Travelling exhibition service. Essay by Ksawery Piwocki.

Individual Artists

Artist's writings (arranged chronologically); works about the artist; exhibition catalogues (arranged chronologically).

165 Zurich. Kunstgewerbemuseum. *Das Plakat: 400 neuere Plakate aus 25 Landern.* Apr. 18–May 17, 1953. 48 pp., illus.

166 Zurich. Kunstgewerbemuseum. *Meister der Plakatkunst.* May 13–July 19, 1959. 70 pp., illus., bibl.
Foreword by Hans Fischli; essay by Willy Rotzler. Biographies.

167 Zurich. Pro Helvetia Foundation. *The Swiss Poster: Traveling Exhibition.* 1950. [72] pp., illus.
Text in German, English, French, Spanish, Italian, and Portuguese.

Herbert Bayer

168 Dorner, Alexander. *The Way beyond 'Art'—the Work of Herbert Bayer.* New York: New York University Press, 1958. 154 pp., illus.
Originally published New York: Wittenborn, Schultz, Inc., 1947. 244 pp., illus.

See also bibl. 14

Aubrey Beardsley

169 *The Posters of Aubrey Beardsley.* [London: Francis Marsden, 1968.] 10 color plates.
A re-issue of the ten posters in original size and color, printed by photo-lithography as were the originals. Unbound. Limited to 500 sets, each poster numbered.

170 Reade, Brian. *Aubrey Beardsley.* New York: Viking Press; London: Studio Vista, Ltd., 1967. 372 pp., illus., bibl.
Introduction by John Rothenstein. Emphasizes drawings but includes posters.

Peter Behrens

171 *Ein Dokument deutscher Kunst: die Ausstellung der Künstler-Kolonie in Darmstadt, 1901.* Munich: Bruckmann, 1901. 47 pp., plates in folio.

172 Cremers, Paul Joseph. *Peter Behrens: Sein Werk von 1909 bis zur Gegenwart.* Essen: Baedeker, 1928. 168 pp., illus.

173 Hoeber, Fritz. *Peter Behrens.* Munich: Müller & Rentsch, 1913. 249 pp., illus., bibl.

See also bibl. 50

Joseph Binder

174 *Colour in Advertising.* London and New York: The Studio, 1934. 29 pp., illus.

Pierre Bonnard

175 Martini, Alberto. "Gli inizi difficili di Pierre Bonnard," *Arte Antica e Moderna* (Bologna), July–Sept. 1958, pp. 255–279, illus.

176 Rewald, John. *Pierre Bonnard.*

New York: The Museum of Modern Art, 1948. 151 pp., illus.

177 Roger-Marx, Claude. *Bonnard lithographs.*
Monte Carlo: Editions du Livre—André Sauret, 1952. 184 pp., illus.
Introduction by Claude Terrasse.

178 Soby, James Thrall, James Elliott, and Monroe Wheeler. *Bonnard and His Environment.*
New York: The Museum of Modern Art, 1964. 116 pp., illus., bibl.

Will Bradley
179 *Will Bradley: His Chap Book.*
New York: The Typophiles, 1955. 104 pp.

A. M. Cassandre (Adolphe Mouron)
180 *Publicité.*
Paris: Charles Moreau, n.d. 4 pp. plus 49 plates.

181 *Le Spectacle est dans la Rue.*
Montrouge: Draeger Frères, [1936?]. [20] pp. illus.
Introduction by Blaise Cendrars.

182 *Posters.*
St. Gall: Zollikofer, 1948. 118 pp., illus.

183 New York. The Museum of Modern Art. *Posters by Cassandre.* Jan. 14–Feb. 16, 1936. 16 pp., illus.
Foreword by E. M. Fantl.

184 Paris. Musée des Arts Décoratifs. *Exposition A. M. Cassandre.* Oct. 1950. 22 pp., illus.
Preface by Bernard Champigneulle.

See also bibl. 105, 160

Walter Crane
185 Konody, Paul George.
The Art of Walter Crane. London: Bell, 1902. 147 pp., illus.

See also bibl. 19

Jules Chéret. See bibl. 15

Walter Dexel. See bibl. 56

Hans Erni
186 Rosner, Charles. *L'Oeuvre graphique de Hans Erni: Integration de l'art et des techniques.*
Geneva: Cailler, 1957. 27 pp., illus.

Karl Gerstner
187 *Designing Programmes.*
New York: Hastings House, 1964. 96 pp., illus.
Introduction by Paul Gredinger. Translated from *Programme entwerfen,* Teufen: Arthur Niggli, 1964.

John Heartfield
188 *Photomontagen zur Zeitgeschichte, I.*
Zurich: Kultur und Volk, 1945. 101 pp., illus.
Includes essays by Alfred Durus, Wolf Reiss, and Louis Aragon.

189 Herzfeld, Wieland. *John Heartfield: Leben und Werk.*
Dresden: VEB Verlag der Kunst, 1962. 353 pp., illus.
Appendix includes writings.

190 Selz, Peter. ''John Heartfield's photo-montages,''
Massachusetts Review (Amherst), 1963, pp. 309–336, illus.

191 Stockholm. Moderna Museet. *John Heartfield, Deutsche Akademie der Künste DDR: Fotomontör.* Sept. 1–Oct. 1, 1967. 48 pp., illus. Chronology.
Catalogue by John Heartfield, Bengt Dahlbäch, and Olle Eriksson.

Armin Hofmann
192 *Graphic Design Manual: Principles and Practice.*
New York: Reinhold Publishing Corp., 1965. 172 pp., illus.
Preface by George Nelson.

Ludwig Hohlwein
193 [Designs for Posters]. [192?].
Album on deposit in New York Public Library, consisting of 32 mounted plates.

194 *Ludwig Hohlwein and His Work.*
New York: H. C. Perleberg, 1922. 40 plates (150 illus.).

195 Frenzel, Herman K., ed. *Ludwig Hohlwein.*
Berlin: Phönix, 1926. 71 pp., illus.
Foreword by Walter F. Schubert. German and English text.

Herbert Kapitzki
196 Seitz, Fritz. *Posters: Herbert W. Kapitzki, Almir Mavignier.*
Washington, D.C.: The Library of Congress, 1964.
Catalogue of exhibition sponsored by the German Arts Council.

E. McKnight Kauffer
197 "The poster and symbolism,"
Penrose's Annual (London), v. 26, 1924, pp. 41–45, illus.

198 *The Art of the Poster: its Origin, Evolution, Purpose.*
New York: Albert & Charles Boni, 1928. 190 pp., illus., bibl.

199 "E. McKnight Kauffer, Poster Designer,"
Portfolio (Cincinnati), no. 1, 1950, pp. [24–39], illus.

200 New York. The Museum of Modern Art. *Posters by E. McKnight Kauffer.*
Feb. 10–Mar. 7, 1937. 24 pp., illus.
Notes by the artist; foreword by Aldous Huxley.

See also bibl. 70, 105

Takashi Kono
201 Ito, Itsuhei. *Takashi Kono—Designer.*
Tokyo: Nichikawa Book Store, 1956. 83 pp., illus.
Captions and text partly in English. Insert: "Flowers of Nerve," by
T. Hijikata (4 pp.).

El Lissitzky (Eleazar Markovich)
202 Küppers-Lissitzky, Sophie. *El Lissitzky: Maler, Architekt, Typograt, Fotograf.*
Dresden: VEB Verlag der Kunst, 1967. 407 pp., illus., bibl.

Charles Rennie Mackintosh
203 Howarth, Thomas. *Charles Rennie Mackintosh and the Modern Movement.*

London: Routledge and Kegan Paul; New York: Wittenborn, 1953.
357 pp., illus., bibl. Chronology.

Almir Mavignier. See bibl. 196

William Morris
204 Sparling, H. Halliday. *The Kelmscott Press and William Morris, Master Craftsman.*
London: Macmillan, 1924. 176 pp., illus.

Józef Mroszczak. See bibl. 52, 162

Josef Müller-Brockmann
205 *The Graphic Artist and His Design Problems.*
Teufen: Arthur Niggli, 1964. 186 pp., illus.
Text in German, English, and French. Author's biography, pp. 185–186.

Alphonse Mucha
206 *La Plume* (Paris), no. 197, 1897.
Issue devoted to Mucha.

207 Mucha, Jiri. *Alphonse Mucha: His Life and Art.*
London: Heinemann, 1966. 391 pp., illus., bibl.
Translated from: *Alfons Mucha, Meister des Jugendstils.*
Prague: Artia Verlag, 1965.

208 Reade, Brian. *Art Nouveau and Alphonse Mucha.*
London: H. M. Stationery Office, 1963. [64] pp., illus.
Second impression, 1966. First issued for exhibition at Victoria and
Albert Museum, May–Aug. 1963.

209 Zurich. Kunstgewerbemuseum. *Alphonse Mucha (1860–1939): Plakate und Druckgraphik.* April 19–May 13, 1967. 28 pp., illus., bibl.
Preface by Erika Billeter. Biography, artist's memoir.

Pablo Picasso
210 Czwiklitzer, Christophe. *290 Affiches de Pablo Picasso.*
[Cologne?]: Chez l'Auteur Art—CC, 1968. 304 pp., illus.
Catalogue raisonné. Preface by Jean Adhémar; introduction by
Charles Péraussaux.

211 Foster, Joseph K. *The Posters of Picasso* (new enlarged edition).
New York: Grosset & Dunlap, 1964. 35 pp., illus., plus 48 plates.
First edition, New York: Crown Publishers, 1957.

See also bibl. 51

Paul Rand
212 *Thoughts on Design.*
New York: Wittenborn, Schultz, Inc., 1947. 159 pp., illus.
French and Spanish translations, pp. 137–159.

213 Kamekura, Yusaku, ed. *Paul Rand: His Work from 1946 to 1958.*
New York: Alfred A. Knopf; Tokyo: Zokeisha, 1959. 132 pp., illus.
Text in English and Japanese.

W. H. C. Sandberg (Willem Sandberg)
214 *Experimenta Typographica II.*
Cologne: Galerie der Spiegel, 1956. [58] pp., illus.

Ben Shahn
215 *Love and Joy About Letters.*
New York: Grossman Publishers, 1963. 79 pp., illus.

216 Soby, James Thrall. *Ben Shahn: His Graphic Art.*
New York: George Braziller, 1957. 139 pp., illus., bibl.

John Sloan
217 Sloan, Helen Farr. *The Poster Period of John Sloan.*
Lock Haven, Pa.: Hammermill Paper Co., 1967. [32] pp., plus 12 plates.

Théophile-Alexandre Steinlen
218 Crauzat, E. de. *L'Oeuvre gravé et lithographié de Steinlen.*
[Paris?]: Societé de Propagation des Livres d'Art, 1913.
Catalogue; preface by C. Roger-Marx.

219 Sachs, Hans J. ''Théophile-Alexandre Steinen,''
Der Cicerone (Berlin), June 1924, pp. 483–494, illus.

220 New York. Charles E. Slatkin Galleries. *Théophile-Alexandre Steinlen.*

Oct. 18–Nov. 16, 1963. [96] pp., illus., bibl.
Preface by Alan M. Fern. Essay by Alain de Leiris.

221 London. Arts Council of Great Britain. *Steinlen: An Exhibition of Drawings, Engravings and Book Illustrations.* n.d. 30 pp., illus., bibl.
Notes taken from May–June 1953 exhibition, Bibliothèque Nationale, Paris.

Henri de Toulouse-Lautrec
222 Joyant, Maurice. *Henri de Toulouse-Lautrec, 1864–1901.*
Paris: Floury, 1926–1927, 2 vols., illus.
Vol. 2 on graphic arts. Edition reprinted by Arno Press, New York, 1968.

223 Julien, Edouard. *The Posters of Toulouse-Lautrec.*
Boston: Boston Book & Art Shop, 1966. 97 pp., illus.
Translated from the French, Monte Carlo: André Sauret, 1966.

224 Lassaigne, Jacques. ''Henri de Toulouse-Lautrec: His Complete Oeuvre of Posters,''
Graphis (Zurich), no. 30, 1950, pp. 174–182, illus.

225 Natanson, Thadée. ''Devant les affiches de Lautrec,''
Arts et Métiers Graphiques (Paris), Mar. 15, 1937, pp. 9–18, illus.

226 Baltimore. Museum of Art. *Toulouse-Lautrec: Posters and other Lithographs from the Collection of Mr. and Mrs. Nelson Gutman.* Apr. 17–June 3, 1951.
36 pp., illus.
Foreword by A. D. Breeskin; introduction by Lincoln F. Johnson, Jr.

227 New York. The Museum of Modern Art. *Toulouse-Lautrec: Paintings Drawings, Posters, and Lithographs.* Mar. 20–May 6, 1956. 48 pp., illus.
Preface by Andrew C. Ritchie. Chronology by Anne Hecht.

Jan Tschichold
228 *Asymmetric Typography.*
New York: Reinhold Publishing Corporation, in co-operation with Cooper & Beatty, Toronto, 1967. 94 pp., illus., bibl.
Translation by Ruari McLean of revised edition of *Typografische Gestaltung,* Basel: Benno Schwabe, 1935.

229 *Die neue Typographie.*

Berlin: Verlag des Bildungsverband der deutschen Buchdrucker, 1928. 240 pp., illus., bibl.

230 *Typografische Entwurfstechnik.*
Stuttgart: Wedekind, 1932. 24 pp., illus.

231 "The Typography of Jan Tschichold,"
Modern Graphic Design (Louisville), Spring 1957, 32 pp., illus.
Special issue with essays by Tschichold, Mildred Constantine, and Noel Martin.

Henry van de Velde

232 *Geschichte Meines Leben.* Hans Curjel, ed.
Munich: R. Piper, 1962. 545 pp., illus.

234 Hammacher, Abraham M. *Le Monde de Henry van de Velde.*
Antwerp: Edition Fonds Mercator; Paris: Librairie Hachette, 1967. 353 pp., illus. Translated from: *De Wereld van Henry van de Velde.* Bibl.

235 Brussels. Palais des Beaux Arts. *Henry van de Velde, 1863–1957.*
Dec. 13–29, 1963. 115 pp., illus.
Introduction by Robert L. Delevoy. Essays by Delevoy, R. Verwilghen, L. Lebeer, Fernand Baudin, and Marie Kisselin.

H. N. Werkman (Hendrik Nicolaas)

236 Gruyter, W. Jos. de. "H. N. Werkman, printer of the unknown paradise,"
Delta (Amsterdam), Winter 1959–1960, pp. 28–35, illus.

237 Baden-Baden. Staatliche Kunsthalle. *Hendrik Nicolaas Werkman.*
Spring 1962. [218] pp., illus.
Catalogue by Margot Fuerst et. al. Biography.

238 Groninger. Gronings Museum voor Stad en Lande. *H. N. Werkman.*
Sept. 23–Oct. 7, 1964. 16 pp., illus.
Text by Dr. H. W. van Os.

Piet Zwart

239 Jaffé, H. L. C. "Ein Pionier funktioneller Typografie: Piet Zwart,"
Neue Grafik (Zurich), June 1961, pp. 2–19, illus.
Text in German, French, and English.

240 Müller, Fridolin, ed. *Piet Zwart.*
New York: Hastings House; Teufen: Arthur Niggli, 1966. 112 pp., illus.
Text in German, English, and French.

Index

Page numbers in italics denote illustrations.